THE BOOK OF GENERAL KNOWLEDGE BOMBS

Amazing Facts, Oddities and Curiosities
For Knowledge-Thirsty Minds

BILL O'NEILL

ISBN: 978-1-64845-127-0

DON'T FORGET YOUR FREE BOOK

CONTENTS

INTRODUCTION

The world is a strange place.

That's probably pretty obvious to anyone who's lived on Earth for more than five minutes, but sometimes we lose track of just how weird and wonderful our planet (and the people that live on it) can be.

There's so much happening in human history at any given time that it can be easy to overlook some of the more interesting chapters in history.

This book will take a look at everything from Egyptian painting recipes to the nuclear age, and beyond. Some of it might be strange, some of it might be unbelievable, but *none* of it will be boring!

Each chapter has several stories in it - all of them are true! They are sure to be entertaining and illuminating. If there was ever a companion for random trivia, then this book would be it. In these pages, you'll find everything from ancient history (like smelly emperor robes and frozen mummy shoes) to the Space Race and more. Even seemingly mundane topics like food and the clothes we wear are full of interesting facts and little-known trivia.

And while it's no secret that the world of entertainment is, well, entertaining, you'll have a new appreciation for just how fascinating it can be.

There's sure to be something within these pages that will grab the attention of even the most seasoned trivia enthusiast.

If you need some rapid-fire points of interest, each chapter has a section at the end full of neat little factoids that ask, "Did you know?" And we're willing to bet that you didn't!

So, dive right in - pick something that catches your attention and see if you don't find yourself flipping through the whole book before you're done. This book will have you spouting trivia anecdotes with the best of them. More importantly, it will make history fun and accessible. Hopefully, you'll find something that sparks your interest and can act as a jumping-off point for a quest for more knowledge.

CHAPTER 1:
THE ANCIENT WORLD

THE EMPEROR'S
SMELLY CLOTHES

The word "emperor" probably conjures up visions of decadence and luxury, of fine goods and beautiful palaces. Roman emperors certainly lived up to this image, surrounding themselves with beautiful things and wearing only the finest clothes. They were so iconic that the very idea of royalty wearing purple began with them, a tradition that continued for centuries. There was an unseen aspect to their iconic purple robes, however: that beautiful purple, known as *Tyrian purple*, came at a heavy cost…, mostly to the nose.

Before the invention of chemical or synthetic dyes in the 1800s, all fabric had to be dyed with natural ingredients. Purple was always a tricky color to make, and it usually relied on grape skins left over from making wine. This dye was known as *lie de vin*, and it mostly made purples that came out closer to pink than a rich purple. However, there was another way, and it was all thanks to the Murex snail.

There were actually several different species of snail referred to as Murex, but they were all in the same family. What set these little guys apart from other dyeing methods was that, unlike plant-based dyes, the color they produced got richer and bolder when it was washed and exposed to sunlight. They could make a huge variety of colors from a red so dark it was almost black to the iconic purple robe favored by the emperor himself.

The downside was that making this dye was smelly…, *extremely* smelly. The snails would be harvested from the Mediterranean

Sea and transported to small villages far, far away from anything else. The snails' shells would be cracked, and the snails would be alternately boiled and put into ceramic vats to ferment for weeks, months, or even years depending on what color was being extracted. The smell was so bad that it was forbidden to create the dye anywhere even close to a big city. It was eye-watering, nose-shriveling, and stomach-churning.

Still, it was considered such an important industry that the recipe was kept secret up until the fall of Constantinople in 1453!

THE TEENAGER THAT ONCE DEFEATED CAESAR

Cleopatra is probably one of the most famous names in all of Egyptian history, if not the world. There's hardly a person alive who doesn't know at least the basics about her life, and even more likely, her death too. However, for all the well-known stories about Cleopatra, there's one part of her life that's relatively unknown: She had a younger sister who had a life just as full of intrigue and drama as Cleopatra!

Arsinoe IV was the fourth daughter in Ptolemy XII's family. When he died, he left the Egyptian throne to his son, Ptolemy XIII, and his elder daughter, Cleopatra. He wanted them to be joint rulers, assuming that they would be stronger together. His wish did not come true, however - the younger Ptolemy decided that he wanted to rule alone and caused Cleopatra to flee to Alexandria. Julius Caesar sided with Cleopatra and told them that Cleopatra would be ruling with her brother as her father had wished. Meanwhile, Arsinoe would be given Cyprus to rule with another brother, Ptolemy XIV.

Being exiled in all but name to a small island was *not* what Arsinoe wanted. She escaped from Alexandria and wasted no time in taking the Egyptian army for herself. Her first order was the execution of Achillas, who had previously been commander of the army. She put herself in the top spot. Much like Cleopatra, Arsinoe had been given a good education, and she put her talents to good use. In fact, she was such an effective strategist that she soon had Caesar himself on the run! After Arsinoe's army built walls and barricades to cut off his escape, he was trapped in Alexandria. He became so desperate that he removed his famous purple cloak and armor so that he could dive into the bay and swim to a Roman ship.

Eventually, Arsinoe was captured and taken to Rome. Even though it was customary to execute prisoners, Caesar allowed Arsinoe to live. He had her taken to the temple of Artemis in modern-day Turkey, where she lived relatively peacefully. Cleopatra, however, was not happy with this arrangement. She thought that Arsinoe was still a threat - and she may have been right, for her younger sister had certainly proved that she was an effective leader. So, Cleopatra persuaded Marc Antony to have Arsinoe executed on the steps of the temple itself, which many people were unhappy about.

The truly remarkable thing about Arsinoe was that she was only 15 at the time she led her uprising!

THE DEADLY TOMB
OF QIN SHI HUANG

The idea of a hidden tomb full of traps and treasure really sparks the imagination, especially if it's also got a reputation for being cursed. For the tomb of Qin Shi Huang, the possibility of a curse seemed credible – well maybe?

Qin Shi Huang was the first emperor of China and founded the Qin dynasty. He's perhaps most well-known for ordering the construction of the Great Wall of China and his truly massive tomb which housed the famous Terra Cotta Army. His tomb was so big that it's estimated that it took 16,000 workers two years to complete it!

The Emperor needed a big tomb so that there would be enough room for him to take many treasures to the afterlife. In addition to the Terracotta Army, there was an incredible amount of jewelry, fine cloth, and even replicas of palaces so that he might live comfortably in the afterlife. The tomb had to be safe from anyone who might want to plunder it for its riches, so immediately upon completion, the workers who had labored to build it were executed so that they couldn't give away its secrets.

There were many measures taken to protect the Emperor's hoard and final resting place, including crossbows that could be tripped by someone attempting to break in. Perhaps most important to the tomb's well-being was that it quickly gained a reputation for being cursed: if anyone attempted to break into it, they would sicken and die. This reputation, plus all of the deadly traps as well as the fact that the tomb was partially built into the base of a mountain, meant that it survived relatively unscathed for centuries.

But what caused the rumors of the curse? Sima Quian, a famous Chinese historian who lived about a century after Qin Shi Huang, said that there were 100 rivers of mercury within the tomb. If this was even remotely true, then it would certainly account for people who attempted to break into it sickening and dying.

When modern researchers began excavating the tomb after its discovery in 1974, they were surprised to see that the Emperor's resting chamber was still undisturbed. When they began inserting probes to assess the safety of excavating it, they were even more surprised to learn that there were high quantities of mercury in it - sometimes even as high as 100 times the normal rate! It seems that Sima Quian's description of the tomb was at least partially correct.

Ironically, it is likely that mercury killed Emperor Qin. He was sick at the time of his death and was probably given medicine that had mercury in it, which poisoned him. Now he's buried surrounded by the toxic metal!

THE CURRENCY OF MESOAMERICA: CHOCOLATE

It's pretty safe to say that chocolate is one of the most beloved foods on Earth. There's a variety of ways to eat or drink it these days, with something to fit almost any taste. It's also a global flavor, being eaten on every continent and grown in many countries. Before it became an intercontinental sensation after the colonization of the Americas, it already had centuries of history.

The peoples of Central and South America had been harvesting cacao since at least 1750 BCE. After the pods were harvested, the beans would be extracted and prepared. The most common way of preparing it was for the seeds to be dried and ground into a powder to later be mixed with water. This chocolatey drink was then poured from one vessel to another to make it frothy and well-mixed. Additional ingredients, such as ground and powdered peppers or vanilla, could be added for an additional kick. The Aztecs preferred to drink it cool, while the Maya preferred it hot.

This drink was so important that the cacao bean took on religious significance. The Aztecs believed that Quetzalcoatl had been struck down by the other gods for daring to give humans the knowledge to create the cocoa drink. They also saw a parallel in the extraction of the cacao beans with their human sacrifice rituals in which the heart was removed. Some people in Central America even added achiote to the drink so that it would turn red and look like blood.

For all their love of cacao, however, the Aztecs did not have the means to grow it themselves. Cacao beans became a highly prized trade good, so much so that they quickly evolved into a form of currency all of their own! Not only could goods or food be bought with them, but they were also sometimes used to pay wages. As with any currency, counterfeiters quickly began to circulate fake cacao beans. These were frequently carved and painted pieces of wood or avocado pits, which are definitely not as tasty as chocolate!

ÖTZI'S SNOWSHOES

Much of the past remains a mystery to us today, even with our excellent research methods and technologies. One way to learn more is by studying the dead, mummies in particular. The word "mummy" usually conjures up images of ancient Egypt, but mummified bodies can be found in a variety of places all around the world. One of the most famous non-Egyptian mummies is Ötzi "the Ice Man," as he is affectionately known.

Ötzi was found in the Alps in 1991 after lying in the same spot for nearly 5,000 years. What was truly remarkable about Ötzi was that much of his clothing and possessions survived the millennia; most organic things, particularly clothing, degrade pretty quickly in most environments. Because Ötzi was frozen, this prevented a lot of decay. This allowed scientists to study and learn from him, including what he was wearing when he died.

Footwear specialist Petr Hlavacek undertook the task of recreating the shoes. He used only tools and materials that were available to Paleolithic people, including tanning methods to create the leather. The shoes were made using bearskin for the soles, deerskin for the upper, and cowhide strips to lace them together. Additionally, there was a net inside the shoe that held dried grass for insulation. Though initially met with some skepticism, Petr convinced some modern mountain climbers to test the shoes.

Surprisingly, they outperformed even modern shoes. The bearskin leather provided excellent grip, while the thin deerskin hide shaped well to the leg and flexed nicely. Most importantly, the grass used for insulation kept the climbers' feet surprisingly warm. Because the shoes were so soft and flexible, this allowed more of the surface of the foot to come into contact with the ground, which meant that climbing was easier. They were so effective, in fact, that a Czech shoe company wanted to buy the rights to manufacture and sell them.

Move over, designer brands - perhaps Ötzi's furry shoes will be the next big trend in footwear!

THE NOT-SO-MONGOLIAN ARMY OF THE MONGOLIAN EMPIRE

The Mongolian Empire was the largest contiguous empire in all of human history. From relatively humble beginnings, the horsemen of the Mongolian steppe would go on to rule an empire that included China, part of India, the Levant, and all the way into the Middle East. Their influence was great, with a large trading network that allowed goods from Asia to reach Europe in greater numbers than before. This includes the famous Silk Road, which became the main artery for trade with the region for centuries.

But how did a bunch of rural horsemen transform themselves into such a fierce and effective fighting force? Well, their leader Genghis Khan understood from an early age the importance of information, particularly from outsiders. He encouraged foreign traders to visit his burgeoning kingdom, not only to encourage economic growth but also so that he might learn more about prospective lands to conquer.

Unsurprisingly, the Great Kahn continued to use this strategy when his conquest began. When an area was conquered, he would recruit the best military leaders and strategists to his own army then put them and their talents to work. This was true of the soldiers as well. Once a location fell under Mongol control, they could join the "winning team" and fight for the Kahn. This was encouraged, as it not only kept the Mongols' numbers replenished, but it also kept rebellions down. Additionally, they established an empire-wide communication service made up of relay riders so that information could be quickly spread to the rest of the empire.

Bearing this in mind, it's no wonder that the Mongols became such a uniquely capable fighting force. Not only did they have their famous prowess with cavalry, but they also had experts that gave them everything from explosives to new armor and weapon designs. They also taught them how to build siege equipment, and the most efficient way of doing so - they could build it on-site, as needed, from local materials.

Since they had such a wide network for gathering information, the Mongols also knew exactly how to instill the utmost fear into their potential targets. They would tie branches to the back of their horses to make bigger dust clouds as they approached a city or settlement; tricks like this would give the appearance of their forces being larger than they really were. With their fearsome reputation for fighting and so many clever tactics at their disposal, it's little wonder why so many chose to join the Mongolian army.

DID YOU KNOW?

○ Despite the famous image of Cleopatra using a snake to commit suicide, it was much more likely that she used a needle to inject poison.

○ Emperor Qin Shi Huang's tomb was found by farmers who were hoping to dig a new well.

○ The merchants who traded in cacao beans were so valued that they became a protected group, frequently traveling with soldiers to protect them.

○ It was originally thought that Ötzi may have been killed as a part of a sacrifice ritual, but evidence now points to him being a murder victim.

○ Despite their reputation as fierce conquerors via violent conflict, a lot of cities chose to surrender peacefully instead of facing the Mongolian army.

CHAPTER 2:
FOOD

BEER, THE DRINK THAT BUILT ANCIENT EGYPT

The ancient Egyptians contributed many things to the world, including truly impressive monuments, art, and mathematics. Their civilization lasted for thousands of years and spanned numerous countries and went on to inspire many other civilizations that came after. If you were to ask someone what the Egyptians' great kingdom was built on, they might say, "sandstone," "a strong military," or maybe even "the Nile's regular flooding." While all of these are true enough, there's something that may have been even more important to the building of their civilization: beer.

Grain in general was really important to the Egyptian diet. Most of their meals were centered around bread and other baked goods. Bread was not only cheap and filling, but it could also be used in place of silverware. Grain was also used to make various kinds of filling and nutritious porridge, which was needed to fuel all of the physical labor demanded by the pharaoh. It should be noted that the species of wheat that was grown in Egypt at the time was fairly hard to work with, requiring a lot more processing than the modern varieties do. It took a lot of work to get the nutritious grain ready to eat and when it was, it was hard on the teeth.

However, the importance of beer cannot be overstated. There were many different recipes from all corners of the kingdom that gave a variety of flavors. There was even a goddess, Nephthys, dedicated to the brewing of beer! Wages could be paid in beer or grain, with more skilled workers receiving more.

Now, if you're imagining a pharaoh kicking back and putting his feet up at the end of a hard day with a glass of frosty beer, that's not entirely accurate. This wasn't any beer that you might recognize: It was thick and sludgy, more like a beer smoothie than today's watery drink. It was drunk from special vessels, usually with long reed straws to help filter out any residual seed husks. It may even have been a bit sweeter than modern beers, as honey is listed as an ingredient in some recipes.

This thick, sludgy beer did have a distinct advantage - it was highly nutritious and filling. Equally important was the fact that it had a quantity of alcohol in it. Since germ theory was still some centuries off, drinking water could be pretty unsafe to consume at times. It is, however, pretty safe to say that beer was an integral part of Egyptian life and culture.

THE CENTURY-LONG STOMACHACHE

Sometimes it's pretty easy to take for granted that, when we pick some food off the grocery store shelves or eat it at a restaurant, it will be safe to eat. Instances of mass food poisoning are so rare these days that they're major news events. This wasn't always the case, however; the idea that there should be a government body to safeguard our stomachs from the perils of unsafe food is much more recent than you might think.

In the 1800s, America was growing fast. The population was experiencing a boom, partly because so many people were immigrating from other parts of the world. Most people were working very hard, physical jobs, so they needed a lot of food to keep working. This put a lot of pressure on the farmers and food manufacturers - , they had to produce a lot of food, but they also still wanted to make as much money as they could. To do so, they sometimes resorted to putting things in good that weren't…well, really all that safe. This included things like chalk or paint to make milk look thicker and higher quality than it really was, or minerals like copper to make canned vegetables look greener. Other times, they would use meat that was old and spoiled for canning.

If you weren't wealthy enough to afford fresh food and vegetables that came directly from a grower, you'd likely have to eat some of this so-called "adulterated" food. The effects of these additives weren't well-known, or even studied at all. This led to many people referring to this time as the "century-long stomachache."

Chief Chemist in the United States Department of Agriculture, Dr. Harvey Wiley, who had long studied chemistry, believed that these unsafe practices were harmful, and he set out to prove it. The problem was, how to do so? Luckily, besides being a brilliant researcher, Dr. Wiley understood the importance of another tool at his disposal: public relations. In 1902, he recruited healthy young men who would be given "impure" food to eat, and then the effects would be recorded. This study helped illustrate exactly how dangerous this food was - if healthy, strong, young men were falling ill or writhing around in pain with stomach bleeding after eating the stuff, what would it do to children?

To lobby for food safety legislation, Dr. Wiley enlisted the help of President Theodore Roosevelt, who had seen first-hand how terrible the meat canning was whilst in the army, and culinary expert Fannie Farmer. He also encouraged women to join the cause, as they could use their domestic influence to change minds. Thanks to Dr. Wiley's efforts, new regulations were put into place to keep consumers healthy and safe.

THE COCKENTRICE, A KING'S IMPOSSIBLE MEAL

When it comes to royal appetites throughout history, there are a lot of strange and unusual dishes. Palace cooks had to get really creative to keep the monarch and their court happy, especially since meals were important not just for diplomacy and socializing, but as a form of entertainment. The more elaborate a monarch's dinner table was, the more wealthy and powerful the monarchy would appear to be.

This was especially true for the Tudor dynasty. They had come to power after the Wars of the Roses, and their claim to the throne was still considered shaky. Therefore, in addition to military might, they began a campaign to impress through other means as well, and meals would be no different.

Now, it's important to remember that during the 15th and 16th centuries, there was still a pretty strong belief in mythical creatures. The world wasn't fully mapped yet, and it seemed like every day there were tales being brought back from explorers of strange and unusual animals. You could even say that mythological animals were "trending" across Europe - there was even a thriving market for "unicorn horn" (which was really just a narwhal's tusk more often than not).

So, how did a Tudor king impress his dinner guests? By serving up one of these creatures for dinner, of course! There was just one problem: These animals weren't real, so how does one get cooked? Well, that's where the creative kitchen staff came into play. One of the most show-stopping dishes was the *cockentrice*, a dish that was meant to resemble the cockatrice…, well, sort of.

A suckling pig's upper body would be sewn to the lower half of a chicken or turkey, or vice versa so that nothing is wasted. After these were sewn together, it was basted with a mixture of saffron to give it a golden color as well as to add flavor. Alternatively, it could be covered with gold foil to really make it golden. Sometimes the insides were also covered with gold that it appeared to be gold the whole way through. Additionally, the stuffing would be made with the most expensive ingredients to be found, including slivered almonds, saffron, pepper, ginger, pine nuts, and sugar or honey. The cockentrice was meant to impress, inside and out!

THE SAUCE THAT RULED THE ROMANS: GARUM

It seems like humans have always loved adding sauces to their food. Today, we have all sorts of options, from ketchup and Tabasco to honey mustard and ranch. During the Roman Empire, however, there was one sauce that reigned supreme: Garum. It was put on *everything*!

But what is garum? Well, to put it bluntly, it's the juice that is left from a barrel or vat of salted fish that has been left to ferment…, for months, maybe even years. Sometimes this liquid would be thickened to a paste so that it could be used as a preservative all of its own. Given how much time and work went into making garum, it's hardly surprising that the best stuff could cost ridiculous amounts of money.

Beyond being important to the Roman diet, it seems that garum and the making of it were important to the Roman economy, too. There's some evidence to suggest that the whole reason they conquered some coastal areas around Gaul (modern France) and Hispania Baetica (modern Spain and Portugal) was simply so that they could have access to the species of fish needed to make garum, such as anchovies. In fact, it seems that the very best, most desirable garum came from Baetica. The ill-fated city of Pompeii also relied on garum production for much of its wealth too.

Of course, anyone who's ever been around a pile of rotting fish knows that the smell is unpleasant, to say the least. Unsurprisingly, this meant that there were strict laws about where garum could be manufactured, namely outside of any towns or cities. Private citizens were forbidden from brewing the stuff in their own homes unless they lived on a large, spacious estate. As such, garum was generally made out in the countryside or on the coast, somewhere with plenty of fresh air.

It's natural at this point to wonder what, exactly, garum was used for, and the answer to that is *everything*. It was used much like we use sauces today, to add flavor while cooking or on finished dishes. However, it was also used in ways that might be surprising. Besides acting as a flavoring, it was touted as having medicinal properties and was used for everything from animal bites to removing unwanted hair and freckles. Some people recommended it for stomach ailments, and Roman author and naturalist Pliny noted that sometimes it was watered down and drunk for a variety of purposes. It was even used as a flavoring on some desert dishes, like pears in honey - and you thought pickles and ice cream was a strange combination!

The closest equivalent today is Soya Sauce or Worchester Sauce.

POTATO PROHIBITION

There's a serious argument to be made that potatoes are one of the most versatile foodstuffs on the planet. So much can be made from them, from chips and fries to alcohol, even candy! Given that they're so ubiquitous, found on every continent these days, it might come as a surprise that, at one point, a lot of people were afraid of potatoes - very, *very*, afraid. People were so afraid that there were even laws against growing or consuming them in some countries!

Potatoes are part of the *nightshade* family, which includes tomatoes, but also, and more well-known for a lot of centuries, the deadly nightshade plant and all of its poisonous cousins. When the potato was initially introduced to Europe from the Americas, people flat-out refused to eat it, believing that it would be deadly. In fact, in France, most people wouldn't even give them to their pigs to eat! This was a real problem because, unlike grains, potatoes can endure a lot of hard growing conditions and are pretty resistant to a lot of diseases. More importantly, they're denser in calories than grains.

There was one man who saw the potential in potatoes: Antoine-Augustin Parmentier. He was fully convinced that potatoes could be a lifeline to France in the event of bad harvests. The problem was how to convince everyone that they were not only safe but good to eat. He embarked on a plan of potato propaganda that had a multistep agenda.

The first part of his plan was to prove that potatoes were safe. He began to advocate for their use to feed invalids and prisoners, people for whom food was always in short supply. While this approach proved his theory, and he received scientific prizes, the community assumed he was attempting to poison people and booted him out! Back to the drawing board.

The next step was to attempt to make potatoes fashionable - after all, if something is in fashion, it doesn't matter how absurd it is, people will want it. Parmentier began hosting lavish dinners where potatoes featured as the main ingredient. He invited noteworthy guests, such as Benjamin Franklin and many French nobles. He even went so far as to gift Marie Antoinette and Louis XVI potato blossoms, which they wore as an accessory.

While all of this was unfolding, there was still a general suspicion about potatoes that could not be overcome. That was when Parmentier had a stroke of pure genius. On a small allotment of land given to him by the king, he began to grow potatoes. Around this garden was a very impressive-looking fence, complete with a sturdy gate. He even went so far as to pay armed guards to stand around the perimeter; however, the guards left at night. Strangely, potatoes and potato plants began to disappear from the garden, which was exactly what Parmentier had wanted! It was as true then as it is now: People always want what they can't have.

VODKA IN SPACE

Even though the ideological conflict between the United States and the Soviet Union was known as the Cold War, it was in real danger of heating up several times. With such a serious conflict that could have global consequences, there really wasn't much time for levity or even attempts at comradery. There also wasn't really anywhere that could be considered truly neutral ground, except for one place: space.

On July 17, 1975, the American space shuttle *Apollo* docked with the Russian spacecraft *Soyuz*. The entire purpose of the mission was to help ease relations between the two superpowers. Tensions were naturally very high, as both nations had a lot of suspicion toward each other. It was worried that the astronauts and cosmonauts might have trouble communicating, be impeded by their cultural differences, or that the different types of shuttles wouldn't be able to dock together properly. This proved to be unfounded, however, as both crews shook hands and exchanged warm, congenial greetings. The Russians even announced that they had a gift for the Americans!

To give full context, it's important to understand that NASA has always had a very, very strict policy about alcohol in space. Beyond concerns that it might inhibit reflexes or impair judgment, it's a practical concern - no one wants a flammable liquid floating around the space shuttle! There's also a pressure concern, as the very act of getting to space puts a lot of force on any food packing, never mind one that has bubbles. It was only very recently that any sort of alcohol was permitted on American space stations, and even then, it was usually only for scientific study.

That being said, the Russian policy was technically the same - in theory. In practice, cosmonauts had been smuggling alcohol into space from day one. Their methods for doing so were quite ingenious, from using hollowed-out books to hide a bottle to losing weight so that they could hide bottles inside their spacesuits. It was a very poorly kept secret.

So, when the doors between the space shuttles opened, with the whole world watching via a live broadcast, there was a lot of pressure to keep things friendly. It was a bit of an awkward situation, then, when the Soviet cosmonauts offered the Americans a tiny bottle that was labeled "VODKA." The Americans knew that they had to be friendly, but all of their supervisors at NASA were watching—what to do? Well, astronaut Vance D. Brand took a swig in the spirit of good relations…, only to realize it was actually borscht!

DID YOU KNOW?

○ The meals served aboard the *Titanic* were so luxurious and delicious that even the third-class meals were considered to be as good as second or even first-class meals on other ships.

○ Marie Antoinette never said, "Let them eat cake." This is a mistranslation of what she was reported to have said, "Let them eat *brioche*," which she also never said - it was purely propaganda.

○ During the Irish potato famine (1845–1852), the Choctaw nation collected $170 to send to Ireland. This was only 15 years after they had been forced to relocate on the Trail of Tears, and they understood what it was to face starvation.

○ Ergot, a type of mold that grows on rye bread, has often been blamed for the strange experiences blamed on witchcraft that led to the Salem Witch Trials. However, if there *had* been an outbreak of ergotism, more in the community would have shown symptoms than the group of girls who were the accusers. They also wouldn't have expressed remorse, as many did afterward.

○ Carrots weren't originally orange - they were purple, white, or shades of blue. They were bred by the Dutch specifically to have that color, and it became favored because it stays a nice color in soups and stews.

CHAPTER 3:
THE THINGS WE WEAR
- CLOTHING AND MAKEUP

WHALEBONE
(NOT REALLY) CORSETS

Is there a piece of clothing more misunderstood than the corset? Probably not. From being accused of causing deformed skeletons to breathless descriptions of how they kept women constantly on the verge of fainting, the humble corset has had to put up with a lot.

Corsets, as they were known in the 19th century ("stays," "bodies," and "jumps" before that), were mostly for support, not for pulling in the waist so tight that women couldn't breathe. Clothing in the 1800s could be quite heavy, so it was important to have a sturdy foundation.

Probably one of the biggest myths surrounding corsets is what they were made of. The term "whalebone" conjures up images of giant ribs taken from marine mammals and used to construct rigid cages that contorted women's bodies into the desired shape. This is a bit of a misunderstanding, though: Whalebone isn't a bone at all!

During the 19th century, whales, specifically sperm whales, were used for many different things. Whaling was a huge industry, supplying ingredients for everything from cosmetics to lamp oil. Whaling ships were sort of like floating factories, able to hunt and begin processing the whales right out at sea. What they didn't harvest, at least most of the time, were the bones. That's right, even the term "whalebone" is incorrect! Whalebone is actually *baleen*, or that bristle-like filter that some whales have in their mouths. These bristles are covered with keratin, so they're very strong but also very flexible.

This baleen is what was used to give corsets their structure. Before whaling became so efficient, cords, reeds, and even straw were used to give bodices their support. Baleen had an advantage, though, in that it was flexible enough to give that iconic hourglass shape. Additionally, baleen reacts to warmth, so it would form and shape to the wearer as it came into contact with body heat. This ensured a comfortable fit.

Since baleen had many material properties that wouldn't be duplicated until late in the 20th century, it was used for a lot more than just corsets. Anything that needed to be flexible and strong could be made from baleen, including umbrella frames, baskets, and whips.

POCKETS:
A GIRL'S BEST FRIEND

It might be hard to believe, but the humble pocket has quite a storied history, particularly in women's clothing. For such a small, hidden part of our clothing, it sure does have some interesting stories to tell.

The key to understanding a lot of the pocket's history is to understand that our modern idea of pockets has only been around for less than 100 years. Before women's clothing changed to be thinner and more form-fitting, pockets were a separate garment that tied around the waist in the 1700s and earlier. These pockets could be (and frequently were) quite large, able to hold a wide variety of items. The outer layers of clothing would fold over or have slits cut into the sides so that women could reach in and access their copious pockets.

Unfortunately, having these pockets tied on loosely could result in them getting snatched. Court records show that women kept *everything* in their pockets: sewing supplies, shawls, extra socks, money, cosmetics, books, journals, even whole loaves of bread sometimes. And you thought your mom's purse had an outrageous amount of stuff in it!

These large pockets were sometimes also used in the commission of crimes. They were obviously easily used for petty theft, but occasionally criminals got more...*creative*. Take, for instance, the case where a woman in rural England claimed to be able to give birth to live rabbits. She would have on only a chemise or thin undergarment to show a large stomach as if she were truly pregnant and would retire to her bedroom. An assistant would follow her in later and then would emerge holding a live rabbit. What the astonished crowd didn't realize was that the assistant was actually just smuggling the critter in her pocket and had taken it out when she entered the room. With that kind of creativity, it's probably a good thing they didn't have access to our giant tote bags!

WIGS, HIGH HEELS, AND ROUGE: MASCULINE VICES

Beauty standards have always been evolving, and the concept of an "ideal man" is no exception. In fact, many of the clothes and accessories that we think of as being "feminine" were originally common for men to wear or even actually invented for men's use.

Take the wig, for example. While people have been using extra hair and padding to achieve a desirable hair-do nearly since the dawn of civilization, full, styled wigs were first invented for men. These weren't any ordinary wigs, either, but luscious, perfectly curled locks that hung down past the shoulders. It could take hours to style it properly, and they were really valuable - so valuable that they were sometimes the target of theft!

High heels are another item of dress that was favored by men for centuries. Pants or trousers that went all the way to the ankle weren't popular until the 1800s, which meant that men's calves were almost always on display. Having long, elegant calves was greatly desired, so men would wear high blocky heels to emphasize their legs. Since silk stockings were a status symbol, this was a good way to show off their wealth. This also gave them extra height, which helped them to look more powerful at court or in government positions.

Even makeup was commonly used by men, particularly during the 1700s. There was a surprisingly wide variety of items available, including powder, rouge, and lash and brow darkeners. A clean, youthful face was the desired look, so many men would apply powder and rouge to achieve this. For those that had scars, usually from smallpox, they could use tinted creams, or even apply little velvet patches called *mouches*. These little black patches, precursors to today's face stickers, had a language all of their own, with different shapes having different meanings.

It might be hard to imagine, but our ancestors were very concerned with being as beautiful as possible and used all the tools at their disposal to be as lovely as possible.

X-RAY HAIR REMOVAL

Humans have seemingly always wanted to find ways to remove unwanted hair. It seems like almost every day there's a new beauty treatment that guarantees smooth, hairless skin. Methods have included things like waxing, shaving, plucking, and even…, X-rays!

The discovery of X-rays in the late 19th century would have long-reaching consequences, especially for healthcare. A forgotten part of the early years of X-ray technology, however, is their use in the beauty industry. A man named Leopold Freund was researching X-rays, and he discovered that exposure to them resulted in hair loss. He was hoping to find a new treatment to help people with copious body hair. His findings would have a huge impact - but not in the way he had intended.

As women's fashion became more revealing, women of Western Europe and the United States began to shave their legs. This was time-consuming, especially at a time when more women were entering the workforce or simply being allowed to go out unchaperoned and do what they wanted. Much like today, women wanted a way to permanently remove their hair so that they could get on with their lives.

There was suddenly a cracking trade for X-ray machines for use at beauty salons, doctors' offices, and even at home (for those who could afford them). Women would sit and hold up their faces or legs to the machines, receiving a massive dose of X-ray radiation. Their hair would indeed fall out, but it would have long-term health effects.

These health effects weren't understood until the 1940s, at which point machines were taken off the market. Stories about women developing cancer or tumors circulated, but even so, people would still seek out this treatment in the name of beauty. This treatment was so popular that a study in the 1970s showed that out of all the radiation-based cancer diagnoses up to that point, up to 35% of them were caused by X-ray hair removal.

GOVERNMENT-ISSUED LIPSTICK

During World War II, the United States government mobilized everything they could to help with the war effort. This included recruiting women to important industries — Rose the Riveter is an iconic symbol of this all-hands-on-deck approach. Women were also encouraged to join the armed forces via organizations such as the Women's Army Corp, or WAC.

Though the work was hard and sometimes dangerous, it was still an appealing prospect for many women. They had the opportunity to travel, enjoy a degree of independence that was hard to find on the home front, and learn new and valuable skills. There was another benefit to joining up too: Each soldier was given a set of makeup as part of their uniform.

War-time rationing had hit every industry, including cosmetics. While makeup itself wasn't rationed, it did become very expensive - it was hard to justify buying lipstick when it was more important to buy food. However, the United States believed that it was an important way to keep up morale, so they made sure that their women soldiers were perfectly styled with red lips as they marched into the field. Women working in bomb factories were likewise supplied with makeup to help them keep their spirits up and to make sure that they were camera-ready at all times.

The WAC makeup kit included powder, mascara, lipstick, and various face creams. Other items could be included too, such as eyeliner and blush, but this wasn't consistent. In addition, their uniforms were designed to be attractive as well, with tailored jackets and fitted skirts. This was in direct contrast to other countries that used female soldiers, such as the Soviet Union. In the Red Army, women were given bulky, shapeless one-piece outfits, which had originally been designed for men.

Despite their delicate appearance, General Douglas MacArthur praised the WAC as his "best soldiers" and hardest workers.

LACE: THE FORGOTTEN STATUS SYMBOL

Throughout history, people have distinguished themselves from others in numerous ways. Nowadays, if we see someone wearing a lot of gold or jewelry, it's pretty safe to assume that they have a lot of wealth or status. This wasn't always the case, however. Something a lot softer and frillier used to be the swag of its day: lace.

In the time before industrialization and mass-produced clothing from factories, everything had to be made by hand. This included any embellishments for clothing too, such as buttons, ruffles, and of course, lace. Lace was very time-consuming to make, and also took a lot of skill. In fact, a common charitable scheme was to set up "lace schools" in rural areas so that poor girls could learn this valuable skill to make more money. Depending on how complicated and intricate the pattern was, a single square inch of lace could take hours to make and cost a week's wages for an average laborer.

With this in mind, it's little wonder that lace quickly became a status symbol for the very rich. The frothier lace that one had on their cuffs or collar, the wealthier that person appeared to be. This was true for items like shawls, caps, and tablecloths, too. Whole communities could come together to make enough lace for something important, like an altar cloth. Men would even sometimes give their wives or sweethearts lace as a present instead of jewelry because it cost about the same!

Because of how expensive lace was, an industry sprang up of laundresses who specialized in caring for lace. It would have to be removed from the rest of the garment and washed in a special way that preserved it. Many laundresses came up with recipes to keep the lace white and beautiful, including everything from soapwort plants to milk. It would also have to be dried carefully, being gently folded up and pressed between towels or drying cloths. When it was clean and dry, women would store their treasured lace carefully wrapped in tissue paper and kept somewhere safe and dry. It's hard to imagine something so seemingly simple being treated like it was as valuable as gold!

DID YOU KNOW?

○ Contrary to popular belief, Queen Elizabeth I didn't slather her face in thick white paint. The recipes that she used produce a translucent, very subtle foundation that makes skin glisten under candlelight (but can still be pretty toxic). The most popular white foundation, called ceruse, was made out of white lead and vinegar. Concoctions used to bleach freckles and treat blemishes often included ingredients such as sulphur, turpentine and mercury.

○ During World War II, fabric was needed so badly for uniforms and bandages that it was common for people to make clothing from flour sacks. The flour companies caught onto this and began printing beautiful patterns on their sacks to entice customers.

○ Since medieval shoes had soft soles, it meant that people had to walk differently than we do today - they put their toes down first. This was especially true for people wearing shoes with long pointy toes.

○ King Louis XIV of France began a fad of having bright red heels on his shoes. He declared that only aristocrats and members of court in royal favor were allowed to wear them.

○ Though synthetic fiber seems like a modern invention, it was actually under development as early as the 1930s as a means of replacing more expensive silk.

CHAPTER 4:
ENTERTAINMENT

JOSEPHINE BAKER:
SINGER, DANCER, SPY

When it comes to ground-breaking artists of the first half of the 20th century, there's no shortage of people from which to choose. It's a testament to how great she was that Josephine Baker looms large over most of them. Born into humble circumstances in St. Louis in 1906, she would go on to take the stages of Europe by storm after being rejected by American theaters.

But there's more to this songbird than meets the eye. Though she would achieve great fame through her singing and dancing, and even a film career, her most important work was largely outside of the public eye - or hidden in plain sight. When World War II broke out, Josephine Baker was recruited by the French intelligence services to act as an information gatherer. Because of her fame, Baker had access to high-ranking foreign officials, and she was adept at charming information out of them.

Many of them underestimated her because of her race and the fact that she was an entertainer, known for humor and dancing rather than intellect. This was a clever misdirection on her part, for Baker had always been very clever and good at reading people - she knew how to get German army officers and Japanese officials to underestimate her and let secrets slip. She could also go on tour to a variety of locations because of her status as an entertainer, allowing her to pass information along.

After the war was over, Baker received many honors for her work during the war, including being named a Chevalier of the French

Legion of Honor, the Resistance Medal, and the Croix de Guerre. She took up the mantle of Civil Rights activism in the United States, having long suffered from discrimination whenever she wanted to perform in her homeland. She was honored by the NAACP for her continued work and gained many famous and powerful friends during this time that also helped to further the cause for equal rights.

In 1963, during Martin Luther King Jr.'s March on Washington, Baker was invited to speak, which she did while wearing her French service uniform. She was the only woman who was permitted to take the podium that day.

Josephine Baker was such an effective speaker and leader that after King's assassination, his widow, Coretta Scott King, invited her to become the new head of the Civil Rights Movement. Though it was tempting, Baker declined because she wanted to be with her adopted children.

HOLLYWOOD VS. NAZIS:
FORGOTTEN CONGRESSIONAL HEARINGS

The Golden Age of Hollywood (about 1927–1960) produced a lot of cultural touchstones that are still important today. Artistic expression was paramount and ushered in a golden age of cinema. Movies of the 1940s were understandably patriotic, with a focus on keeping morale up and people united during a turbulent time.

This wasn't always the case, however. The United States was initially reluctant to get involved in World War II. A lot of political and social groups were vehemently opposed to going to war again, especially on such a scale - after all, many of them could vividly remember the horrors of World War I. In fact, there was even a Nazi party that was active in the United States, headed by Fritz Kuhn.

Many people in Hollywood, both those of Jewish descent and gentiles alike, didn't like what they were seeing happening in Europe. When it began to spread to the US, many studios, directors, and actors took action. Movies that painted Nazis in a poor light began to be released in quick succession, such as *Confessions of a Nazi Spy* and *The Great Dictator*.

These movies were seen as dangerous because they could sway public opinion, and the US government didn't want to get pushed into war. The US Senate in particular was determined to nip this problem in the bud, especially after Fritz Kuhn sued Warner Brothers studio for their film *Confessions of a Nazi Spy*. The Senate, led by Senator Gerald Nye, opened hearings on September 9, 1941, regarding the alleged push for intervention in the war in Europe by Hollywood, emphasizing that many of the studio heads and directors were Jewish and clearly had an agenda.

The biggest problem, besides the fact that there were Nazis active in the US, was that public opinion was quickly swinging in the other direction already. By 1941, the Nazis already controlled most of continental Europe, and it was making the American public uneasy. The pictures coming out of Europe were really brutal too, which roused a lot of people to think taking action was the right thing to do.

The commission quicky ran out of money and wasn't approved for more. Their pursuit became a moot point anyway when Japanese planes dropped bombs on Pearl Harbor on December 7th of that year.

HEDY LAMARR: MORE THAN THE MOST BEAUTIFUL FACE

Once considered the most beautiful woman in the world, Hedy Lamarr had a storybook Hollywood career. Her face was like a moving work of art, a muse come to life. Beneath her good looks, however, there was a brilliant mind at work. It's thanks to her that we have one of the most useful technologies of the modern age: Bluetooth!

Hedy Lamarr had always had an interest in technical things. Whenever she had a break between filming scenes, more often than not, she was drafting schematics for new inventions. Some included an improved stoplight and even a capsule that could create a fizzy drink if dropped in water. Lamarr was married to an arms dealer from Austria, and she found that she really liked attending meetings with him - so much so that she became an even better salesperson for his weapons than he was!

It was during one of these meetings that Lamarr learned that the Navy needed a better guidance system for torpedoes. This would be very relevant in just a few years when World War II broke out. The idea that had the most traction was to use radio frequencies, but there were concerns that an enemy ship or submarine could hijack this and turn the torpedo around. Lamarr , with the help of a musician friend, realized that the answer was frequency hopping, or having the radio frequency change in sync with both the torpedo and the boat.

Excited by her realization, Lamarr began work immediately. She consulted with electrical engineers to see if the idea could work practically. Her invention came to life in 1942, and she had it patented under her legal name. Lamarr was sure that the Navy would want to use her invention. She was disappointed, however, when they rejected it: They claimed it was due to size, but Lamarr felt convinced it was because she was a woman, and because she was so pretty - she couldn't possibly be a genius if she was beautiful.

Lamarr's fears were confirmed when she was told that she would be better off selling war bonds because she was so famous, and the soldiers liked her. It seemed the world only wanted her to be a pretty face, not to also have an amazing mind. When she began to age and was no longer seen as a potential money spinner, she retired. Hedy Lamarr lived in seclusion. She died in 2000 before she could see her invention become appreciated the world over. Her frequency-hopping technology is what allows Bluetooth to work.

DISNEYLAND'S THE WONDERFUL WIZARD OF...BRAS

Disneyland has no shortage of amazing attractions that delight people of all ages. The theme park seems to always be on the cutting edge of entertainment, with millions of guests visiting the park each year. It's known for its wholesome entertainment, safe for the whole family. This wasn't always the case, however: On Main Street, there was an emporium that sold - bras.

Yes, really.

In fact, the shop labeled "Intimate Apparel, Brassieres, and Torso Lettes" sold more than just bras - there were also corsets and various items of lingerie available to buy. The store was kitted out to look like a Victorian-era shop, complete with costumed staff. There was also a revolving stage in the shop where the Wonderful Wizard of Bras would educate guests about the history of underwear. There were samples on display from all the way back in the 1800s, showing the evolution of undergarments.

It wasn't all just educational, though. It was largely an advertising space and shop for the Hollywood-Maxwell Brassiere company. There were all sorts of modern garments featured, from new styles of bras to petticoats to help women achieve that famous 1950s look. A lot of guests weren't entirely sure what to make of all this, as the older generation felt it was a little distasteful. Older men tended to take off their hats when they entered the shop, while the younger men and women were a bit more casual about the whole thing.

The shop didn't last long, though and was removed by January 1956. The storefront is still visible on Main Street (without the signs); however, the interior was taken over by the China Shop next door, which has expanded. Even though there's a sign that advertises Fargo's Palm Parlor, offering palm readings, the door is locked. The interior is still part of the China Shop, and the signs are just clever advertising that make it look more interesting for park visitors. It's debatable if palm readings are more or less interesting than a miniature museum dedicated to underwear, however.

ROCK AND ROLL
BUILT THE CT SCAN

Modern medicine is full of technology that seems almost miraculous. The ability to view the inside of a human body without having to slice it open is a huge boon (and a huge relief). One of the most important devices that allows us to do this is the CT scan, or "computed tomography." While there's no shortage of scientists and researchers to thank for this amazing machine, there's also one more unexpected thing to thank: rock and roll.

In the 1950s, the record company EMI (originally Electric and Music Industries) boasted a pretty robust catalog of artists. Founded in 1931, EMI had always focused on more than music, being one of the biggest producers of the gramophone. This would set the stage for the company to have a long-standing interest in technology generally. By the 1950s, they distributed music for some of the world's most famous artists, including Nat King Cole, Frank Sinatra, and even Elvis' international recordings. Naturally, this meant they were pretty flush with cash.

This financial winning streak would increase exponentially in the 1960s, as they would go on to sign the Beatles, Pink Floyd, and later, Queen. These were all artists who sold extremely well, and EMI saw record profits. But what to do with all of these piles of money?

EMI turned back to its roots and interest in new technology. There was a growing demand for more advanced medical care brought about by the growing strength and number of computers. This was a brand-new idea, that computers could help doctors not only do mundane things like manage patient records but also actually assist in the diagnoses and care of patients.

So, EMI gave Godfrey Hounsfield, a researcher who worked for the company, essentially a blank check to research whatever he wanted. After a lot of testing and some help from the British government, the CT scan was born. Of course, it was known at the time, and for some years afterward, as the EMI scan. The invention was so important that Hounsfield was awarded the Nobel Prize. Forget building a city on rock and roll - medical breakthroughs were built on it too!

TUPAC AND SHAKESPEARE

The rap scene of the mid to early 1990s was defined by very high-profile conflicts, mostly between East Coast and West Coast rappers. A lot of the music produced at the time dealt with violence and the gang lifestyle. One of the most prolific artists making music was Tupac Shakur. His songs were popular hits, known by millions. What is less known is the fact that he was actually interested in classic literature and the performing arts.

While attending high school in Maryland, Tupac was accepted into the Baltimore School of the Arts. This provided a wide education across many different subjects. While there, Tupac studied everything from ballet to classical literature and acting. These were all skills that would serve him well later in his career, providing a wellspring of inspiration. He also noted the similarities between Shakespearean plots and gang rivalries, with the drama and betrayals providing a fertile ground for creativity. Tupac's time training as an actor would also help him develop a strong stage persona and to be comfortable moving about on the stage.

Perhaps most surprising of all, Tupac excelled at ballet. Again, this helped him learn how to use an entire stage for his performances, as well as widening the scope of music with which he was familiar. It would also help develop his sense of rhythm. Besides performing in Shakespeare's dramas, Tupac was so talented at ballet that he was cast in the school's performance of *The Nutcracker* as the Mouse King. Remember, this was a school that centered on the arts, so he was up against some stiff competition!

Though he moved on from the school, Tupac never forgot these early lessons. Most of the media wanted to focus on his tendency to rap about violence and what it was like to grow up in disenfranchised neighborhoods, but this was frustrating to him. He expressed irritation more than once that no one ever wanted to discuss anything else with him, only seeing him as a boy from the 'hood, when he was very concerned about the possibility of peace. No one would ever discuss Shakespeare or any of his other favorite poets or writers during interviews, which only contributed to the image of him as a man obsessed with violence.

DID YOU KNOW?

○ Grace Kelly, later Princess of Monaco, saw Josephine Baker being refused service at the Stork Club in Manhattan. The actress was so enraged by this that she escorted Josephine from the club with her entourage and refused to return. She became one of Josephine's best friends.

○ Shirley Temple, famous for her dancing and acting, was suspected of actually being an adult and not a child at all because she was so talented. This went as far as the Vatican, which sent a priest to confirm that she was actually a child.

○ The Hollywood Walk of Fame is hiding a secret: There's a time capsule under it that was buried in 1990, and it has all sorts of celebrity-donated items. It will be opened in 2060.

○ Disneyland used to publish its own newspaper that covered attractions and human-interest stories called *The Disneyland News*.

○ Though he could not receive credit for it because of contractual reasons, Michael Jackson helped pen the song "Do the Bartman," as sung by Bart Simpson (with Michael Jackson) on the album *The Simpsons Sing the Blues.*

CHAPTER 5:
SCIENCE

THE DEMON CORE

In the early days of nuclear research, the safety protocols that scientists and researchers are obliged to abide by now were seriously lacking. Part of this was down to simply not understanding how dangerous some of the materials being used were, but some of it was also down to not accounting for human error. This would prove to have tragic consequences regarding a piece of plutonium with an ominous name: the Demon Core.

To understand why the Demon Core was so dangerous, it's important to understand that it was always close to the point of becoming supercritical. This means that it would take very little for it to release powerful blasts of neutron radiation. It was this very nature that led to the first tragedy related to this dangerous item.

Scientist Harry Daghlian was working on an experiment regarding neutron reflectors. Basically, he was stacking a set of tungsten bricks around the Demon Core in different configurations and monitoring which would cause neutrons to be reflected back at the core most effectively. This brought it to the point of subcriticality many times. While doing this - again with none of the machinery or safety precautions we would expect today - Daghlian dropped one of the tungsten bricks directly onto the Demon Core. This immediately set into motion a chain of critical reactions. He reacted quickly before it could become a massive disaster, snatching up the tungsten brick with his bare hands. Unfortunately, he had already received a fatal dose of radiation and died 25 days later from acute radiation poisoning.

Less than a year later, the Demon Core was involved in yet another fatal accident. A team led by Louis Slotin was working on furthering the principle explored by Daghlian. Instead of using tungsten bricks, he was using perfect spheres, like hiding candy in an Easter egg. He was seeing how close he could bring them together before it went supercritical. However, he was doing this with only a flathead screwdriver, maintaining a tiny gap so that the two halves of the sphere wouldn't meet.

Unfortunately, on May 21, 1946, Slotin slipped, and the two halves met. There was a bright flash of blue light, and Slotin immediately used the screwdriver to flip the top half of the sphere off. In the next few seconds, he ordered everyone in the room to remain where they were so that they could calculate who had received the worst of the radiation, and they could inform doctors who needed help the most. Slotin himself would die only nine days later, but his body shielded many of the other scientists that were in the lab with him that day.

THE PRICE OF A SAFE PLACE TO WORK: PHOSSY JAW

When most of us head to work for the day, we naturally assume that there will be protocols and rules in place that keep us safe. This wasn't always the case, however - workplace health and safety is an invention of the 20th century. It was also an uphill battle, with a lot of the push coming from a surprising place: matchstick makers.

Throughout most of history, something as simple as lighting a candle or oil lamp was a multistep process. Matches didn't really exist like they do today, and those that were around were notoriously hard to light or burned wildly. Improvements were made throughout the 19th century, and in 1836, Janos Irinyl invented matches that burned evenly and uniformly.

The problem with these was that they used white phosphorous. Because there were no workplace regulations to protect the workers, this led to serious health problems. Factory owners paid women, especially girls, less for their work, so a large portion of their workforce was under the age of 18. These workers began to develop a condition referred to commonly as "phossy jaw," which was a slow, painful rotting of the jaw. There wasn't really any treatment available except for the removal of the lower jawbone, which caused problems all on its own. The matchgirls had enough of this in 1888 and launched a strike. They suffered hunger and abuse in the push for safer working conditions.

It would take decades for their efforts to have effect, however, by which time it was too late to help many of them. Bans on the use of white phosphorous swept through Europe in the late 1800s. America, however, was slow to adopt these regulations. In 1912, President Taft signed the White Phosphorous Match Act, which only required those who still used white phosphorous to make matches to register and to pay a tax of two cents per 100 matches. Eventually a ban was placed on its use in the United States as well, and it was mostly thanks to a bunch of brave girls and women who refused to back down.

MONKEY MEDICINE

The ability to care for each other is a defining feature of humans. Over the centuries of our existence, we've developed all kinds of ways of helping one another when we're sick or hurt. Other animals do this too, but we're the only ones that have developed medicine and specialized treatments…, or so we thought.

It's been a mystery for a long time as to when we began practicing what might be deemed "medicine," though it's estimated to have been at least 5,000 years ago. For a lot of our history, medical treatments were limited to natural ingredients, usually found close to where we lived. Even though these approaches seem pretty simple compared to today's standards, they still apparently distinguished us from our other primate cousins.

Scientists have been studying other primates and monkeys to see if they could figure out when exactly the idea of using other substances to treat health problems began in our evolution. The closest they got was observing a variety of animal species that would eat specific things to help with parasites, but this was also always self-administered.

That was until 2019, when scientists studying chimpanzees in Gabon, West Africa. During the study, they were surprised to see that, for 22 chimpanzees that had open wounds of some sort, insects were used 22 times to treat them - in other words, 100% of the time. The chimpanzees were catching insects out of the air, pressing them between their lips, and then placing them on the cut. After a period of time, they would pull the insect back out. Most importantly, they weren't just treating themselves: They were treating each other, too. Mother chimpanzees even treated their babies.

This is significant because it's the first time another animal species, especially a primate besides *homo sapiens*, has been observed medicating another member of their community.

TRAIN TUNNEL DINNER

Imagine that you're an engineer in the Victorian era, and you've been presented with a problem: How do you connect two neighborhoods in London that lay on opposite sides of the Thames, and there's no room in the city to build a new bridge? Surely the easiest solution is to just dig a tunnel, right? However, it's an audacious proposal, given that no one has ever managed to build such a tunnel, especially such a large one, beneath a river that big.

This was exactly the conundrum presented to Marc Brunel and his son, Isambard. This tunnel was desperately needed so that it could connect two sets of docks on either side of the river. This would reduce transit times and make it faster for ships to get loaded and unloaded, which would help with the congested Thames River traffic. It would also help the people of London travel across the city faster, which was good for everyone.

The problem was that this had never been done before. To build the tunnel in the water-logged soil beneath the river, a brand-new machine was built that would shield the workers and take the weight of the tunnel while it was being constructed. This made people nervous, and the general public was skeptical that such a tunnel would ever be safe to use. It also made securing funds difficult, especially after there was an incident where the tunnel flooded.

So, Isambard came up with a solution: He would host a banquet in the tunnel, right next to the construction site. This would prove that the tunnel was safe and keep the public interested. It wouldn't be just any ordinary dinner, either - it would be an elegant, luxurious affair. On November 10, 1827, gentlemen in top hats and ladies in silks and furs descended down a deep shaft to the in-progress tunnel. There were fancy tablecloths and candelabras to help set the mood. A band played as guests arrived and while they ate. The food was of the highest quality, and there was no shortage of liquor available for copious toasts. The guests included government officials and war heroes.

As strange as it might have been to host a dinner party underneath a river, it worked! The people of London were so fascinated that they wanted to come and tour the construction site. The directors guided the curious onlookers to see the machinery in action for a shilling each. This proved a lucrative way to offset some costs, as it's estimated that between 600-800 people came to see it every day!

RADIUM FEVER

People have always liked new things. Whenever a new invention or discovery is made, it seems like we just can't wait to use it for - well, anything and everything! This was also true during the early age of radioactivity, when new materials were being experimented with. Of course, these materials just happened to be radioactive and dangerous, but this didn't stop people from using them for all kinds of strange things. This is how the radium craze began.

Radium was first discovered by Marie Curie and her husband Pierre during their experiments with uranium. In 1910, they found that it was a pure metal. If treated with heat and other chemicals, it glowed a beautiful shade of green. It was hailed as a new miracle substance and was put into everything - and we really do mean *everything*!

It might be strange to think of now, but radium was put into everything from cosmetics and hair products to toothpaste. Radium was the buzzword of the 1910s–1920s, and everyone wanted a bit of it. It was even put into dishes, with promises to give food or water a "healthy" infusion of radium. One of the most popular uses was in Radithor, sometimes known as "radium water."

Eben Byers was the son of a wealthy industrialist and a championship amateur golfer. He was also a big proponent of the power of radium water. After injuring his arm, he was given some by a doctor. Byers fully believed that it was helping him, and he took several doses every day. By 1930, however, it was clear that something was very wrong with him. He was losing weight, his hair was falling out, and then his teeth began to fall out too. The government was increasingly concerned about reports of people getting sick from radium products, and they sent doctors to take Byers' official statement.

Unfortunately, they were too late to prevent Byers from suffering terrible consequences. His whole upper and lower jaw were removed except for a couple of upper teeth, and it seemed like his whole skeleton was just disintegrating. They even reported that there were holes in his skull. He died soon after on March 31, 1932. Although it was reported that he died from "radiation poisoning," it was actually myriad cancers that killed him.

Whatever his cause of death, Byers' body was so radioactive from all of the radium that had accumulated in his bones and organs that he had to be buried in a lead coffin.

THE WILD WORLD
OF MUSHROOMS

If you were to think of impressive things in nature, your mind probably immediately goes to some of the more impressive animals out there, like bears or whales, or maybe even to the giant redwood trees that are wide enough to drive through, or ancient jellyfish. It's pretty unlikely that you'd consider the humble mushroom, or its funky fungi family, worthy of numbering with that crowd. Yet mushrooms are a lot cooler (and a lot weirder) than you might expect.

Let's start with the basics: What *are* mushrooms? Well…,we're not entirely sure. OK, we're *mostly* sure. Despite how they may have been classified in the past, scientists have discovered that mushrooms are actually more closely related to animals than plants. This kind of makes sense, given that mushrooms don't have chlorophyll, the substance that lets plants derive energy from the sun. Also, unlike plants, they expel carbon dioxide, just like animals.

Mushrooms are also way bigger than you assumed. It might be easy to imagine that they're all just small little things growing in the shadows of larger plants, especially when staring down at sliced mushrooms on a pizza, but this is not always true. They can be massive with interconnected networks; what can appear to be several mushrooms is usually just one organism. In fact, the largest living organism in the world is a mushroom that is 3.5 acres wide and over 2,400 years old!

As if that wasn't interesting enough, there are even some mushrooms that can glow. There have been over 80 species of glowing mushrooms identified thus far. The bioluminescence of some species is so strong that it's used as an artificial light source by local people.

Speaking of glowing mushrooms, in the exclusion zone around the former Chernobyl nuclear plant, there grows a species of mushroom known as *cryptococcus neoformans*. This hardy mushroom has evolved a unique adaptation to life in an irradiated zone: Its skin produces large amounts of melanin (the same pigment that makes human skin look darker). This melanin helps the mushroom to convert radiation into energy. These mushrooms are so well-adapted that some of them have even taken to growing in the old cooling towers of the plant - they don't need sunlight anymore because they can use "radiosynthesis."

These amazing fungi might even help humans travel to space. NASA is studying the possibility of extracting the mushrooms' melanin and using it as a means of protecting humans from the radiation of space!

DID YOU KNOW?

○ The common myth that nuclear fallout downwind from a testing site killed John Wayne due to contamination while filming *The Conqueror* is completely untrue. It was actually his huge smoking habit that caused cancer.

○ Even though they look light and fluffy, clouds actually weigh about a million tons because of all the water they contain.

○ On one of Jupiter's moons, Io, there's no water, but the pull of gravity from Jupiter and the dozens of other moons around the planet means that there's still a tide - but instead of it being bodies of water, it's solid rock.

○ Most of Earth's oxygen is produced in the ocean from marine plants.

○ A unique species of silkworm was created when Junpeng Mi gave silkworms the genes from spiders to spin webs. This produced silk that was 6 times stronger than Kevlar when woven together.

CHAPTER 6:
ART

GOT MILK? ER... PAINT?

For as long as humans have been making art, we've also been experimenting with new materials to use in making said art. This is an important aspect of art history because it can help experts identify when pieces of art were made. It also has allowed many famous artists throughout history to create unique recipes for paint so they could achieve a unique look to their art. Oil, pigment, and water are all elements that are pretty expected to be found in paint. However, there's one very, very important ingredient that you wouldn't expect: milk!

Whole milk or just the whey leftover when the fat is separated out (such as when cheese is made) has been used as a base for paints for thousands of years. This type of paint is called *casein* paint. Casein paint has a smoother, more even texture, so painting large areas looks neat and uniform. The protein in the milk bonds with the minerals or other pigments and produces a more vibrant color than just plain water does. The residual fat in the casein will also act as a preservative, so the color in question won't fade.

Milk paint is one of the oldest paints in the whole world. It was used in many cave paintings, such as those in South Africa. Even though humankind hadn't domesticated cattle yet, they would still specifically hunt the beasts to get the milk for this very reason. Some of the artwork that used casein is over 49,000 years old, and still brightly colored!

This is best evidenced by the still-vibrant murals in Egyptian tombs and monuments. The Egyptian climate naturally helps preserve things, being so hot and dry, but the casein paint also did its part. The thick nature of the paint made it a perfect choice for the precise and delicate work needed to create the exquisite motifs and hieroglyphics on display in the tombs of the wealthy and powerful. Additionally, because the paint went on so thick, it would survive someone brushing up against it or even slight chipping. Not only does it do well on walls, but also furniture.

It's not just ancient artists that favored casein, though. Artists such as Vincent Van Gogh used it to preserve their drawings, especially those done in charcoal since it can smudge and brush off the page. Even Andy Warhol liked using casein paint in some of his works. Modern artists are beginning to start using a watered-down milk spray as a fixative or sealant for their work as an alternative to chemical sprays.

TOULOUSE-LAUTREC'S
UNLUCKY BREAKS

The 19th century saw a lot of changes in the art world. There were many new art movements and styles, such as the Pre-Raphaelites and the Impressionists. Even those who worked in classical styles offered new perspectives. Art began to take on a more sympathetic approach to its subject, as well as the relationship the art had with the viewer - instead of creating pieces meant just to illustrate a religious or mythical story, it was sometimes made just to give the viewer an emotional response.

One of the most notable artists who encompassed both new perspectives and sympathy for the subject was Henri de Toulouse-Lautrec. He was undeniably talented from a young age, earning the praise of his tutors. However, it wasn't just pure talent that gave him a nuanced perspective: it was his own misfortunate.

When Henri was 13 years old, he fell and broke his left leg in a fall. This left him stuck in his bed for months while it healed, time that he used to work on his art. A year later, when Henri was 14, he fell into a ditch and broke his other leg, also at the femur. It was likely that he suffered from some sort of bone disease. Breaking his thigh bones while a growing teenager meant that his legs stopped growing. His torso continued to grow as it should, which gave him an unusual appearance. Unfortunately, this led to people mocking him and making cruel remarks about his short stature (he was only 4 feet 8 inches tall).

It was because of this ridicule and being seen as an outsider that Henri de Toulouse-Lautrec developed such a sympathetic eye for other outcasts. He painted the women who worked in the

Paris nightlife with great care, especially those at the Moulin Rouge. He portrayed people otherwise seen as disposable or less than human as capable of joy and tenderness. Despite his fairly privileged upbringing, Henri Toulouse-Lautrec also became a good cook and loved to feed his guests and models delicious meals.

His time living in such an environment took its toll, however. His constant pain led to a lot of drinking, and he contracted chronic diseases. Henri de Toulouse-Lautrec died at only age 36, but his art became renowned for its joyful movement and empathetic treatment of his subjects.

THE MONA LISA'S SECOND CHANCE AT LIFE

It's hard to think of a painting more iconic, more world-famous than the *Mona Lisa*. Her face graces everything from t-shirts to mugs. Millions of people flock to view her every year where she hangs in pride of place in the Louvre. It might be surprising to learn, however, that she was not always such a celebrity. In fact, it was only because of a shocking turn of events that the *Mona Lisa* became such a famed work of art.

For much of its existence, the *Mona Lisa* wasn't really all that famous. The painting was mostly only known to people who extensively studied Da Vinci's works, or other art from the period. In fact, Napoleon had the painting hanging in his bedroom just because there was an empty space the right size. All of this would change on one fateful day in 1911.

In August of 1911, the Louvre was undergoing some renovations. On August 21, the *Mona Lisa* was stolen. The French police scrambled to investigate, even interrogating Pablo Picasso as a possible suspect. There were no clues, and it was a real mystery - it was like it had just vanished without a trace.

The upside of the theft was that the *Mona Lisa* showed up all over the world in newspapers reporting on the theft. This led to the subject's enigmatic face becoming one of the most recognized in the world. It was hoped that all of this publicity would help people to identify the painting if it showed up for sale somewhere.

This was actually how the thief was caught. It turned out that a man named Vincenzo Peruggia had smuggled the painting out of the Louvre one night after hiding in a closet. He had been working in the museum to make framing and glass cases for the paintings, and he didn't like that such a masterpiece was overlooked. He stole the painting, hoping to bring it back to Italy, where he thought it truly belonged. Peruggia wasn't counting on so much publicity, however, and he kept the painting hidden for two years. He only got caught when he attempted to sell it to the Uffizi Gallery in Florence.

Ironically, his plan sort of worked. The *Mona Lisa*, and Da Vinci's work as a whole, gained new appreciation. This humble portrait is now regarded as one of the world's great masterpieces. Of course, now it's well protected behind a thick glass case, a wooden railing, and all sorts of alarms, so it can only be appreciated from a distance.

MICHELANGELO:
ART FRAUD

The art world is a tricky place to find success - anyone who's attempted to make a career out of it knows this first-hand. Not even the artists that we consider to be masters now were immune to this struggle. Though he would go on to become one of history's most well-known artists, Michelangelo faced a great deal of hardship in his early career. In fact, it was only thanks to a forgery that he found success at all.

During the Renaissance, artists were supported by patrons. These patrons were wealthy and powerful men, sometimes also high-ranking members of the Catholic Church. They would essentially support an artist, paying them a salary and funding their living expenses and materials, and in exchange, the artist would create works for them. This would ensure that the patrons had sumptuously decorated houses and gardens to show off their wealth and status.

In 1496, Michelangelo was in desperate need of a patron. Well, actually, he was in desperate need of *any* kind of money. He'd formerly had a patron in Lorenzo de Medici, but he had died in 1492. While Michelangelo still sculpted, true success eluded him. He didn't want to spend his life living in his father's house, so he needed to find a way to make some money, and fast.

Michelangelo created a couple of smaller statues, one of which was *Cupid*. Lorenzo di Pierfrancesco de Medici saw the work and thought it was pretty good…, but he also knew that there was another way to make more money. He advised Michelangelo to scuff it up a bit and make it look like it had been buried for a long time. This done, Michelangelo sold it through his art dealer to Cardinal Riario of San Giorgio, claiming that it was an ancient Roman statue that had been excavated.

The cardinal, however, was not fooled. He knew that it was a fraud, but he wasn't terribly concerned about that. The *Cupid* was beautiful and extremely well-made, and he liked the piece regardless. He invited Michelangelo to come to Rome and work, and his offer was accepted. From this point onward, commissions were never in short supply for Michelangelo. He was so successful that he died with over 50,000 gold ducats in personal wealth, which was more than some princes at the time, though he chose to live simply.

MARIE ANTOINETTE'S REVOLUTIONARY PORTRAIT

In the centuries before the invention of photography, painted portraits were really the only way to see strangers or important figures. These portraits were frequently loaded with symbolism so that they could convey as much information as possible. With this in mind, it's hardly surprising that people put a lot of stock in these portraits. While they might look elegant by today's standards, some of these were quite groundbreaking, scandalous even, when they were painted. One of the most overlooked examples of this is *Marie Antoinette with a Rose* by Elisabeth Vigée le Brun.

Although it seems like a pretty standard portrait by our standards today, it was quite shocking at the time. For starters, le Brun was one of only 14 women admitted to the Royal Art Academy in France out of about 550 artists. That the Queen of France would ask such an unknown artist to paint her was pretty groundbreaking on its own.

However, it's the way that Marie Antoinette was painted that was the real problem. Although she's modestly dressed to our eyes, she's wearing a very modern and controversial dress for the time. The cotton industry was beginning to really take off in Britain and the Americas, which was bad news for the silk weavers of France. The fact that Marie Antoinette chose to be painted wearing a cotton (muslin) dress made it seem like she didn't care about the struggling French weavers.

Beyond this, this style of dress known as a *chemise a la reine* (among others) was pretty scandalous, too. Up until this point, kings and queens wouldn't think of appearing in public in such a simple garment, and certainly not sitting for a portrait so underdressed. Silks and velvets were what the public was used to seeing monarchs in; in comparison to the sumptuous costumes usually worn, the *chemise* looked like Marie Antoinette had been painted in her underwear! In fact, a chemise was the first layer of clothing put on for much of history, worn right next to the body.

The mood was already pretty negative in France toward Marie Antoinette for a lot of reasons, most of them pretty unfair. She had withdrawn from court life, which she always found oppressive, and wanted to live more simply. This portrait, and her fondness for wearing the *chemise a la reine*, was a reflection of that. However, the public was outraged, and the portrait was quickly removed. La Brun hastily painted another version that showed Marie Antoinette in a blue silk dress.

ALTERING REALITY:
PHOTOGRAPH PAINTING

In a world where we can alter pictures through Photoshop, filters, or any other number of tricks, it's pretty easy to assume that before the advent of these programs and apps, photographs showed the unvarnished truth. There's a somewhat-accepted mindset of paintings which is not always true, and photos are true. However, for as long as people have been taking photographs, they've also been altering them.

In the 1800s, altering photographs was a serious business. There were entire manuals printed on it, such as *A Complete Treatise on the Art of Retouching Photographic Negatives: and Clear Directions How to Finish & Colour Photographs* by Robert Johnson from 1898. Everything could be - and was - retouched from hair color to face shape. Skin was smoothed and scars removed. Those iconic tiny Victorian waists? Fake!

The methods for changing photos were naturally different than they are today. The two most common methods were to change the negative or plate before the photo was even printed. This was painstaking work, requiring a steady hand and precise instruments. The pigment would be scraped away from the negative or colored in with dark pencils. After printing, photos could still be altered, which was frequently the case for ladies' waists. These tricks, along with double exposures, were also used to fake the ghostly, supernatural pictures that were all the rage during the 19th century.

This was the practice well into the 20th century, too. Josef Stalin, the infamous Soviet Union dictator, was very picky about how he was publicly depicted. He used altered photos throughout his whole career, not only to enhance his appearance but also to give himself more credence as a leader. For instance, he altered a number of photographs to make it appear like he was regularly supporting Lenin, or even his close personal friend, which was definitely not true.

Perhaps less seriously, Stalin was very concerned with appearing as young and handsome as possible to the Soviet public. To this end, there was a team of people whose their sole job was to alter portraits of Stalin. They would spend hours hunched over with magnifying glasses and scalpels, scraping away pigment from photographs to erase wrinkles and smallpox scars, which sounds way worse than just picking a cute filter on an app.

DID YOU KNOW?

○ One of the most successful art forgers of the 20th century was Han van Meegeren, who reconstructed 17th-century paints and brushes to recreate the look of Vermeer masterpieces. He also added Bakelite to the paint, which gave it the appearance of an old oil painting that had cracked with age.

○ The Olympic Games used to include an arts category, in which artists in a variety of disciplines would produce sport-themed works of art. This category lasted from 1912–1954.

○ Though we think of Leonardo Da Vinci as a bearded old man, he was apparently quite a hottie when he was younger - fellow painter Giorgio Vasari described him as having "great physical beauty" and "infinite grace."

○ Though he is most well-known for his visual arts, Michelangelo was a prolific writer as well. He wrote over 300 sonnets and madrigals (short lyrical poems).

○ Andy Warhol worked as an advertising illustrator before he found success as a solo artist. He would 'cold' call on advertising firms, and when they asked how he was, he would give an outrageous answer like, "I'm having terrible diarrhea," so that they would remember him.

CHAPTER 7:
TRANSPORTATION

WHEN AIRPLANES WERE CRUISE SHIPS IN THE SKY

Airline travel - just saying it will almost always induce a groan these days. Though fast and convenient, it's not always the most comfortable way of traveling. The food tends to be questionable, there's always an inconsiderate seatmate to fight over the armrest with, and it's impossible to stretch your legs. In the early days of commercial airline travel, however, it was a different story. In the first half of the 20th century, traveling by airplane was an *experience*.

For starters, though they may have been smaller than modern jets, airplanes were much more spacious. Passengers had plenty of room to sit, with the larger planes having multiple spaces for passengers to relax in. There were dedicated dining rooms, lounges, and even smoking rooms and bars. The tables were laid with white tablecloths and passengers were served on real china and silverware.

Don't think that they were served lukewarm mush, either - airline food was the last word in taste. In the early days, they would have to pack meals that would keep well, like fried chicken or various cheeses, but this quickly changed. Airlines would hire notable chefs to create meals that would travel well. In fact, there were whole kitchens with a large staff at each hangar that would cook multicourse meals. Some airplanes even had kitchens so that they could cook and serve food right in the sky! Those that didn't have that option would serve roast beef or ham, sliced right in front of the guests from a trolley.

Part of the reason for this food extravagance was because it was the only way that airlines had to distinguish themselves. Railroads had been boasting luxury travel experiences since the 1800s, after all. Adding to this, airline ticket prices were strictly regulated, so the airlines couldn't undercut each other in order to get more passengers. So, they had to rely on the quality of their food. If only that were still true today - a four-course meal on a long trans-Atlantic flight sounds a lot better than a pack of pretzels.

KATHARINE WRIGHT:
THE FORGOTTEN WRIGHT SISTER

The Wright brothers' iconic flight in Kittyhawk, North Carolina is (rightfully) hailed as an important milestone in history, but it's only part of the story. There's another Wright sibling that frequently gets overlooked: their sister, Katharine.

While the brothers were focused on the practicalities of building a flying machine, Katharine was keeping the day-to-day operations running smoothly. She helped oversee the family business so that they would all still have a steady income while the brothers were experimenting. She also took charge of the practical aspects of their enterprise, ensuring that materials and supplies got to where they needed to go.

Perhaps most importantly, she took on the role of essentially a "public relations" officer. Her brothers were very shy and didn't like speaking to the press or important officials. Katharine undertook these responsibilities, being very charming and witty. She was also fluent in French, which was a real boon to the brothers because France had long been seen as the forerunner in aviation. Throughout the 1910s, Katharine did all that she could to support her brothers and make sure that they got the recognition she felt they deserved.

Another woman was also part of the team: Ida Holdgreve. She was hired to do the practical sewing for the fabric coverings on the wings. Katharine helped to document every little detail, ensuring that her brothers' plans were followed precisely. She felt that it was her duty to "safeguard [her] brothers' interests," and she took that duty very seriously.

Katharine's crusade on behalf of her brothers wasn't the only cause that was near and dear to her heart, though. She fought vigorously for women's rights and became a spokesperson on women's suffrage.

RAILWAY MADNESS

Traveling by train probably seems a little old-fashioned to a lot of people today. After all, it's been around for nearly two centuries at this point. There was a time when this wasn't the case, however, and there was a lot of concern about how to travel safely on the railroads. There were all sorts of fears about them from the practical (Should I pack food? What do I do if I need to use the bathroom?) to the..., well, slightly more absurd (Will my eyes pop out of my head from the speed? Will my internal organs get rearranged?).

Thankfully, all sorts of helpful guides were available to help new train travelers feel reassured. There was some advice in there that still applies today, such as making sure that you arrive early enough to the station to find the correct platform. Some of the guides would help you plan a journey, such as the fastest routes or the most scenic. Others contained whole sections on how to avoid con men and pickpockets. However, it wasn't just preparing for travel that was of concern.

On the earlier models of trains, there wasn't much in the way of internal lighting. This led to a lot of concern about what might happen in train tunnels. As a train passed through a tunnel, it would be bathed in total darkness. Unsavory characters would use this opportunity to steal valuables or assault their fellow passengers. Tunnels were a real source of anxiety for a lot of passengers.

This anxiety could reach unprecedented heights. There were even cases of what was dubbed "railway madness." In May of 1889, a man armed with a gun and his fists seemed to just lose his mind as a train chugged along the English countryside. He went wild, flailing about, attacking passengers, and attempting to break the windows. At the stations, as the train paused, he would become calm and reasonable again. This was not the only case of this occurring, and the cause is still not fully understood.

COOKING ON A STEAM CAR, THE ORIGINAL FAST FOOD

Is there anything as quietly enjoyable as hitting up a drive-thru during a road trip? A refreshing drink, some crispy fries - it's an iconic experience, one that's so familiar it seems like it's been a part of our world forever. Yet while the idea of being able to buy food while out and about is nothing new (even the Romans had fast food stands), the idea of having a place to eat while traveling between towns by car is a bit newer than we might think.

For most of the history of human travel, especially in the United States, food would either have to be packed or hunted. This quickly became impractical as interstates were built and Americans took to motoring as a pastime rather than simply as a means of getting from one place to another. Restaurants popped up, but they were few and far between, especially in more rural areas.

So, what were hungry motorists to do? Well, cook something, naturally - right inside their car!

As early cars were steam-powered, they came with what was really just a slightly altered stove under the hood to provide a source of steam. This would have been very familiar to these early drivers because it would look almost identical to the stove they cooked on at home. People would pack things like ham, bacon, or eggs, and cook them directly on the top of the engine. Because the engine would retain so much heat even when not running, it was a very efficient way of doing things.

Car companies quickly caught onto this and began adding new features to cars to help cook more complex foods. A small oven or food warmer was put underneath the seats, which would have the steam from the engine passing around it. This allowed drivers to bake a small loaf of bread, cake, or even a pie while they drove. It also had the added benefit of being a great seat warmer!

This was so popular that there were entire cookbooks dedicated to the art of cooking on a car engine. In fact, when gasoline-powered cars began to quickly flood the market, designers kept this in mind for several years, making the engines flat enough on the top that they could still be cooked on.

THE FIRST TITANIC MOVIE

The sinking of the *RMS Titanic* in 1912 has been depicted numerous times in films, TV, and radio, perhaps most famously in 1997. Even though the incident looms large in our imaginations and love of disaster movies, there is an overlooked, almost completely forgotten film that really kicked off the public's obsession with the doomed ship. It was created in 1912, only weeks after the ship sank. Even more surprisingly, it starred an actual survivor of the ordeal, Dorothy Gibson.

Gibson, already a notable name in the burgeoning film industry, had been in Europe and was recalled to New York by the film studio she worked for, Éclair Film Company. She and her mother managed to make it to the first lifeboat that was lowered into the sea, no. 7. It was clear to the other passengers on the lifeboat that this sensitive artist was greatly affected by the sinking even as it was happening. What was to come next only compounded her suffering.

Movies at the time were generally very short, usually only about ten minutes or so. Newsreels were shown with them, and the public was eager to see anything that provided information about the *Titanic*. An Éclair producer sent out cameramen and tugboats to get footage of the *Carpathia* as it made its way into port, spliced this together with other footage and turned it into a newsreel. This newsreel became a massive hit, and Éclair decided they should take advantage of the fact that they had a bona fide survivor working for them.

Gibson was quickly hustled to a slapdash film set at the end of April, a little over two weeks after the sinking had occurred. She helped to write a script based on her experiences and even wore the clothes that she had been rescued in. Though filming only took a week, it was a grueling experience. Gibson reportedly broke down in tears multiple times while filming but wasn't given time to recover because they had to hurry and turn the film out while the public was eager for anything *Titanic*. The experience was so traumatic that she had a mental breakdown and retired from acting forever.

DID YOU KNOW?

○ Though a pretty mundane sight today, the bicycle had a massive impact on the poor, especially women. It opened up new work opportunities farther from home without the expense of a horse.

○ In the early days of public transportation, buses were pulled by horses and had two levels. Advertisements were put on these buses not just to earn more money, but also for modesty, to hide the ankles of the ladies who were riding on the upper levels.

○ 1902 saw the world's first speeding ticket issued. The driver was clocked going a blistering 45mph.

○ If you were able to drive a car straight up toward the moon and went at 60mph, it would take about four weeks to get there.

○ During World War II, many cars (especially in Britain) were rigged to run on the gas produced by burning coal because of fuel rationing.

CHAPTER 8:
THE HUMAN BODY

INVISIBLE STRIPES

Though human skin comes in an amazing variety of shades, humans tend to be pretty monotone outside of some specific conditions. I'm sure many of us have wondered what we might look like if we had exotic leopard spots or beautiful tiger stripes. Well, wonder no more - your skin is much more interesting than you thought!

Every person has a set of invisible stripes on their skin called *Blaschko's lines,* named after the person who originally discovered them, Alfred Blaschko. He first noted them in the early 1900s. These lines can take a variety of shapes, including swirls, stripes, splotches, and combinations of patterns. The really neat thing about these lines is that they can help predict how some skin conditions, such as eczema or even poison ivy rashes, will spread.

But where do these lines come from? They're sort of like tree rings in a way - only squishier! When humans are developing in the womb, there's a lot of cell movement going on very quickly. Blaschko's lines show how the skin cells developed, coming in waves or layers. They don't follow the path of the nervous or muscular systems, indicating that they are their own, unique phenomenon. Some doctors think that they can be used to predict some skin problems, such as the way skin cancer grows.

Despite some popular rumors, these lines are invisible to the naked eye, even to other animals. They're only visible under a specific UV light. However, some skin conditions do make them partially visible, such as places of hyperpigmentation. They're occasionally detectable via touch, too!

FINGERPRINTS

We've all probably seen enough police dramas at this point to know how fingerprints work, right? They're the ridges at the tips of our fingers that help us grip things, and they're unique to each person - even identical twins have their own distinct fingerprints! They're almost impossible to permanently alter and even harder to completely remove. It seems like they're a constant part of who we are, a marker of our identity.

This is true..., mostly. Fingerprints do develop relatively early in the fetal development cycle, coming in at about 15 weeks, or the third month, of gestation. Until that point, human fingertips are a bit weirder. Before fingerprints develop, fetuses have *volar pads* at the ends of their fingers. These are big, squishy lumps that look sort of like the pads at the end of a gecko's toes.

When the fetus' hands begin to develop into more familiar shapes at about 15 weeks, the more permanent dermis begins to grow. It grows in waves, and the resulting ridges that are formed from these waves become our fingerprints. Because no one develops 100% the same in the womb, all fingerprints are therefore unique. It's a similar process to how lava flows down a hillside and cools, forming strange ridges and bumps.

Not only does this result in unique fingerprints, but also toeprints, palmprints, and even the soles of the feet!

RESURRECTIONISTS

When we go to the doctor these days, we take it for granted that they will just automatically know how our bodies work. It seems like a pretty basic thing, that doctors should just know what our organs look like and what they do. There was a time, however, not that long ago, when this wasn't actually the case, and going to the doctor could be a little more hazardous.

For many centuries, Western medicine was based on the concept of the *humors*, and though they say laughter is the best medicine, this concept didn't have anything to do with jokes. These were the four elements that medical men believed made up all our insides: Blood, black bile, yellow bile, and phlegm. If someone fell ill, it meant one of their humors was out of balance, and steps needed to be taken to correct it.

This system wasn't really ideal, and frequently did more harm than good. In the mid-to-late 1700s, during the Enlightenment, people started wanting to approach life more scientifically. This was especially true for medicine, but the problem was that no one was really sure how a body *actually* worked. The solution was clearly to perform educational autopsies, but it's not like they could just call someone up and order a body to dissect.

Except they could - and did!

The 18th and 19th centuries saw a wave of grave robbing across Europe, especially in Britain. Instead of stealing jewelry, however, these robbers snatched bodies and would sell them to medical schools or private doctors. All sorts of methods were invented to keep the recently buried bodies of loved ones safe, including cages that bolted into the ground and boobytraps involving guns and tripwires.

The most infamous "resurrectionists" were William Burke and William Hare. Together, they murdered at least 16 people staying at their boarding house so that they could sell their corpses. After all, doctors paid more for fresher bodies, so Burke and Hare figured they might as well create some of their own!

PUZZLE-PIECE MEMORIES

Memories are funny things: They can be triggered by anything from a commercial jingle to a smell from our childhood. They can fade with time or be as vivid as the day they were made. Memories are also a bit more complicated than what a lot of people think.

The brain stores and processes information in a lot of different sections. Each section is in charge of a specific part of the body. For example, *amygdala* is the part responsible for emotions. Components of memories are made up of information from all of these different segments. If it's a memory of your grandma's chocolate chip cookies, then there are many different parts to that memory: smell, taste, and maybe even an image of your grandma's kitchen.

All of these pieces of the memory are stored in their respective centers. When you want to remember something and call up a specific memory, all of the pieces are brought together like a jigsaw puzzle. Of course, it all happens so fast that we don't even know that our brain is assembling the pieces of the memory!

The central area that maps where these pieces are stored is called the *hippocampus*. A lot of times, when someone is described as having memory loss, it's due to damage to this central processor rather than the memories themselves - they're still in there but can't be found. Without the hippocampus, it's a bit like trying to navigate a strange city without any kind of map. Memory trouble can also correspond with damage or disease to the frontal cortex parts of the brain, which is also where our ability to concentrate comes from. It's the frontal cortex that sends the orders to the hippocampus to call up the correct memories.

This is part of the reason why sometimes things that we've forgotten, like things from our childhood or things that weren't deemed important enough to turn into long-term memories, can sometimes be triggered randomly.

COCAINE COUGH SYRUP

The history of medications is a long, long, story, with some truly wild and unexpected twists and turns. Perhaps the strangest time for what we would consider medication was the 1800s - an era of new scientific discoveries and a wider understanding of the discipline that would be known as chemistry.

During the 19th century, there were few regulations or industry standards regarding the manufacture and prescription of medication. There also wasn't a formal education required for chemists to dispense medicines and concoctions for much of the century. The pretty open access to some very...*questionable* substances plus little to no oversight meant that chemists, professional and amateur alike, could just experiment to their hearts' content. The products of these experiments frequently became known as *patent medicines* because the chemists could apply for a patent to protect their idea.

This led to perhaps the most unexpected medication: cocaine cough syrup. Many chemists came up with their own blends, which could vary wildly. These cough syrups could contain anything from opium to cocaine or cannabis, plus anything else that the chemist deemed necessary. They were also frequently made from an alcohol base, such as wine, port, or brandy, though some used ethel alcohol. Even if they didn't actually help with the cough itself, these wild patent medicines would at least dull the pain of a sore throat - or just knock someone out!

Interestingly, it wasn't just cough syrup that had hard narcotics such as cocaine in it. Tooth drops infused with cocaine were sold to parents of children who were teething or had other tooth pain as a means of providing some relief. This is because cocaine has a local anesthetic quality; it *would* provide some sort of relief but was obviously wildly dangerous and had negative long-term effects.

THE RUDENESS OF HANDWASHING

Though it's such a seemingly simple thing, handwashing is widely acknowledged as one of the easiest and most effective ways to halt the transmission of diseases. It seems strange now that there was a time when such a clearly effective practice could be seen as controversial, but there was a period during which even the suggestion that hands should be washed was considered rude.

Though there had been a long-standing tradition in many cultures throughout the world to symbolically or ritually wash hands at specific times, it wasn't really understood to be a means of preventing illness. There were exceptions to this, for example, Moses ben Maimon (Maimonides) who, in the 12th century, pushed for frequent hand washing, such as after visiting a sick patient. He didn't know what germs or other pathogens were, but he did have a surprisingly accurate concept of what caused illness: He believed that there were invisible "spores" that could be on hands and make a person ill.

Unfortunately, Maimonides stands out as the exception rather than the rule. Though germs were beginning to be understood in the 19th century, there was great resistance to demanding that doctors wash their hands. Doctors would go from one patient to the next without washing their hands in between. This led to really rampant rates of infant mortality because the doctors would go from handling a patient with a serious illness to helping a pregnant woman in labor.

The main gripe that doctors had with washing their hands was the assumption that their hands were dirty. Doctors were considered gentlemen, frequently coming from middle- or upper-class families. There was a belief that these classes of people were inherently just cleaner and overall "better" than the lower orders. If doctors were gentlemen, then their hands were clean by default. To suggest otherwise could cost another doctor their reputation and career.

Some, however, continued to push for change. Heroes such as Florence Nightingale and Joseph Lister kept up the good fight, and now we can be healthier than ever with just some soap and water!

DID YOU KNOW?

○ Like many other animals, humans have a scent that is unique to each person. The exception to this is identical twins, who smell exactly the same.

○ In addition to unique fingerprints, humans also have unique tongue prints.

○ Despite popular belief, the Catholic Church wasn't wholly opposed to educational autopsies or dissections. Famous artists such as Da Vinci and Michelangelo were given express permission to study cadavers so that they could improve their anatomy.

○ Sneezing can produce "wind" speeds of up to 100mph as phlegm exits the body.

○ Humans lose an average of 1.5lbs every year of dead skin cells, hair, and other bodily elements that we regularly "shed."

CHAPTER 9:
WAR AND CONFLICT

THE ASSASSINATION THAT ALMOST DIDN'T HAPPEN

Most people are aware that World War I kicked off because of the assassination of Archduke Franz Ferdinand of Austria (though there were plenty of other reasons, too). It's such a famous fact that people can repeat it without even really thinking, sometimes without even really knowing what it actually means. For such a famous event, not a lot of people know that it almost didn't happen - several times!

The assassination was organized by members of a Serbian secret society called the Black Hand. Several young men, some not even 18 yet, were recruited for this task. They knew that the Archduke and his wife would be traveling through Bosnia, and they were determined to act. The team of six would-be assassins got into place on the morning of June 28, 1914. They all believed they were committed, prepared, and ready for anything.

Well, sort of.

The first assassin, Mehmedbašić, had been given a bomb to lob at the motorcade that the archduke and his wife were traveling in, but he didn't actually do anything. A second assassin, Čubrilović, was also given a bomb, plus a gun. He also really didn't feel like blowing anyone up, so he didn't. The assassination attempt was *not* off to a good start.

A third assassin, Čabrinović, was stationed across the Miljacka River, and he too, had a bomb. He actually followed through, throwing his bomb and managing to hit the archduke's car...but it bounced right off, landed underneath a different car, and then exploded. Čabrinović was apprehended, and feeling like the danger had come and gone, the archduke proceeded with his day.

The royal couple decided that they would make a slight change to their schedule, to visit the wounded from the bombing earlier in the day. Their route was not properly communicated, and they ended up driving down a street without an escort. The only assassin left who was still armed was Gavrilo Princip -

and the only reason he happened to see them in their car was because he was coming out of a sandwich shop at the exact right moment! It was less of a perfectly executed assassination plot and more of a series of blunders that ended in tragedy.

HELMET NOT REQUIRED (OR PROVIDED)

War has been the driving force for the development of a lot of different types of armor, from the full steel plate armor of knights to today's Kevlar and ceramic plating. As wars have become deadlier, the armor has improved, generally speaking. World War I, considered by some to be the first "modern" war, was particularly deadly. With all of the new weapons that were coming into use, it's pretty easy to assume that there would be no better time to put on a helmet.

Unfortunately, this bit of common sense wasn't really all that common. None of the first countries fighting in the war provided their soldiers with helmets. Most of the men, if they had any headgear at all, were wearing something soft, like wool or leather. These helmets weren't really designed to do much but protect against rain and cold while in trenches; they were useless against guns and mortars. German army helmets included some steel pieces, which could give a small amount of protection, but it wasn't perfect by any means.

Unsurprisingly, there were a lot of fatal head wounds in the first months of the war. This was obviously untenable, so the French War Department began to design steel helmets for their soldiers. The very first designs looked more like bowls than helmets, and many soldiers didn't know what they were supposed to be used for. One very French re-design later, and the 1915 Adrian helmet was born!

The British quickly followed suit, and they began to design steel helmets too. Though the French Adrian helmet was beautiful, colored in bright silver and adorned with decorations, this was deemed far too expensive and impractical by the British. A simpler design was produced by John Brodie, and pretty soon, the British Army had steel helmets too.

This idea took off like wildfire, and helmets have been part of a soldier's kit ever since. Still, it's strange to think of a time when something as simple as a helmet was considered unnecessary *in war*.

LIZZIE, KIRI, AND MANY: PULLING THEIR WEIGHT

Throughout many of humanity's wars, animals have played an integral part. From cavalry charges on horseback to pigeons delivering vital information, from mules delivering ammunition to soldiers to dogs sniffing out bombs, animals have been integral partners to soldiers since time immemorial.

Of all of these brave animal companions, there's one that might be more surprising than any other: elephants! In addition to their more famous Alps-crossing cousins, elephants also served during both World Wars - and not just in Asia, either.

Lizzie was an elephant living in a traveling zoo when World War I broke out. As she was already near Sheffield, she was sent there to help with important war work. Since fuel was so important to the war effort, Lizzie was an invaluable asset because of her great strength, being able to carry or pull as much as a truck. She pulled munitions and scrap metal to and from factories, as well as delivering machinery where it was needed. She became a local celebrity, and also well-known for her great pickpocketing skills, being able to steal snacks right out of peoples' pockets!

Much like Lizzie, Kiri and Many, two elephants that resided in Germany, were likewise put to work in World War II. Once again, since fuel was scarce, especially with Russia cutting off supplies from the East, large animals were called into service. With trucks being required for the military, Kiri and Many began to do the heavy work that trucks normally would. Much like

Lizzie, they began their lives in a traveling show, a circus. They were used mostly for clearing debris left behind by bombings.

Interestingly, all three elephants were sometimes used for more mundane tasks as well, such as plowing fields. Since horses were needed for the war effort, and it could be difficult to get fuel for tractors, a different approach was needed - and elephants proved quite adept at this job too!

THE RIGHT TO BEAR ARMS
IN THE POLISH ARMY

War can sometimes create some strange friendships. Soldiers and their animal companions are no exception - everyone loves a heartwarming story of a soldier or army unit adopting a critter. Not every animal, however, ends up actually becoming a recognized soldier in said army. Corporal Wojtek was a very special exception…, partly because he was a bear.

Wojtek ended up being adopted as a cub by members of what would later become the Polish 22nd Artillery Supply Company. They traveled extensively, from the Soviet Union to Iran and through Northern Africa. During this time, he grew quite a bit, and proved very adept at a soldier's life. Wojtek loved to wrestle with his comrades and would salute when he saw the other soldiers doing so to superior officers. When it was cold, he would help keep his squad mates warm.

Trouble came about when the 22nd Company was assigned to fight alongside the British in Italy. British transport ships strictly forbade pets of any kind, and initially refused to allow Wojtek on board. That was fine - the Polish Army officially recruited Wojtek as a private. He was given everything that all the other soldiers were, including a salary, a rank, and a serial number to identify him. He even got the rewards that other soldiers did: His favorite post-battle treat was a big drink of beer!

Wojtek worked hard, carrying heavy ammunition crates that normally took four soldiers to lift. He watched his fellow soldiers working, and quickly began copying them, stacking ammo crates carefully on the backs of trucks. He even allegedly helped carry massive 100lbs crates of 25-pound ammunition shells, and never dropped a single one. Because of his bravery and service, Wojtek was promoted to the rank of corporal.

After World War II, Wojtek was given a cushy retirement in Edinburgh Zoo, where he was very popular with the public. His old soldier friends would come visit him frequently, and he always reacted very happily when he heard them speaking Polish to him.

TERUO NAKAMURA:
THE LAST SOLDIER IN THE FIGHT

Even if someone isn't a history buff, there are a few facts that are generally agreed upon, like historically important dates. Arguably, some of the most important dates are when wars began and ended. There is consensus about these by pretty much everyone. For instance, everyone accepts that World War II ended in 1945.

Well..., *almost* everyone.

Teruo Nakamura had no notion that the war ended. Now, it should be expected that not everyone is going to get the news at the same time - after all, communications during war can be fraught at the best of times. Sometimes the local geography adds to this problem. It was a combination of these factors that led to Teruo being the last person to surrender after the end of World War II.

He was stationed on Morotai Island, which is near Indonesia. This island was claimed by the Allies, but Teruo and a few others managed to elude them. The island was then abandoned by both sides, except for Teruo and his comrades. They existed together in the jungle. Eventually, he moved away from them and built a hut on his own and lived there for quite some years.

Teruo was not discovered there until 1974, completely by accident. He was rescued and became the last person to surrender in a war that had officially ended almost exactly 30 years earlier!

He retired and was given a pension, but the public thought this wasn't enough for his extensive service, so they raised additional funds for him. Teruo died only five years later, having served almost his entire adult life on the little island of Morotai.

BLACK MARKET GASOLINE
AND HOW TO MAKE IT LEGIT

Wartime rationing is tough for everyone. Modern conveniences are some of the first things to go, and this primarily means gasoline for cars. This was especially true in World War II, particularly in Britain.

Since Britain was cut off from a lot of fuel reserves, as much fuel as possible needed to be conserved for the military. To keep civilians from simply siphoning out gasoline from parked army trucks, a red dye was added to the gasoline so that if a police officer conducted a spot check, it would be obvious that the fuel had been stolen.

People are nothing if not creative, so a whole industry sprang up almost overnight centered around procuring this illicit gasoline and figuring out ways to make it look legitimate. Rumored ideas about how to remove the red dye including crushing up aspirin and adding it to the fuel, or just mixing it with enough civilian fuel to dilute the color. These weren't really all that effective, and a lot of people got caught.

There was one method, however, that proved surprisingly effective. Though many foods were rationed during the war, such as dairy and meat, bread never was. As long as you could afford it, you could buy as much of it as you wanted. This meant that there was a good amount of it out in the public, and it became one of the best ways to filter the red dye from gasoline.

The gasoline would be poured through the center of a loaf of bread, which would act as a filter. Because the dye was organic in nature so that it wouldn't interfere with the way the gasoline functioned in an engine, it was easily absorbed by the bread. It could then be re-bottled or put into a gas canister, and then sold on the black market. The cost of the bread was minimal, and far outweighed the profits made by being able to clean gallons of gasoline so cheaply. Unwittingly, bread had become a tool of criminals!

DID YOU KNOW?

○ George Washington inadvertently started the French & Indian War (1754–1763, a part of the Seven Years' War). He led a surprise attack against some suspected French spies, that were actually messengers. This led to the world's first global war.

○ In 1932, Australia declared war on emus, seeing them as a nuisance and a danger to crops. It was an unsuccessful campaign, and the emu population remains robust.

○ A stray camel once started a war between two tribes in Arabia in 494 by wandering into a neighboring tribe. The lost camel was promptly shot with an arrow, and the Basus War began.

○ During World War II, the Japanese invaded an Alaskan island in 1943 in order to take over a listening post. The US counter-invaded later that same year with nearly 35,000 troops…, but the Japanese had already left!

○ Jack Churchill was the only British officer to always be armed with a broadsword, longbow, and bagpipe during World War II. He was extremely proficient with all three, and frequently used them all while charging into battle.

CHAPTER 10:
THE WILD WEST

WHERE THE CAMELS ROAM

Ah, the iconic wildlife of the American West: Buffalos, herds of mustangs, coyotes..., camels. Yes, really - camels! Though it might seem strange to believe, there was indeed a time when camels roamed the plains and deserts of the western United States.

In the mid-19th century, the United States began using camels to transport supplies and ammunition around the more inhospitable parts of the country. There could be days, sometimes even weeks, between food and water stops depending on the weather and the seasons. This was too much for a lot of horses, so it only seemed reasonable that camels be used instead. The War Office allocated $30,000 to purchase and import camels, and they did just that, bringing about 75 of them to the United States.

The camels proved pretty useful, navigating the rough terrain and terrible heat and cold of the desserts with ease. They were able to carry a good amount of cargo and required very little in terms of upkeep. All in all, it seemed like a win for everyone involved.

Unfortunately, not everyone was pleased by this prospect. Mule breeders were *not* thrilled at the news that the Army would be using camels for transportation. For decades, mule breeders had been supplying the army with mules for pulling artillery, transporting cargo, and delivering ammunition - in other words, most of what the camels were now going to be used for. So, mule breeders put a lot of pressure on the War Office to abandon the project.

The government didn't need much incentive to comply: The Civil War had broken out in the meantime, and by 1863, some of the camels were simply turned loose to roam the frontier. They were spotted by settlers sometimes, giving rise to all kinds of local legends. Others were sold at auction, and some found their way into service in the Confederate Post Office. Some even found their way all the way to Mexico. After that, they began being spotted in the wild less and less, but the legends persisted about strange, hairy beasts that roared and were 30 feet tall!

THE DENIM RUSH

Blue jeans are such a ubiquitous part of the American wardrobe that it's hard to imagine a time without them. For such an iconically American piece of clothing, it may be surprising to learn that it actually has quite international origins.

Denim, or "jean" has its earliest origins in Italy and France, being a fabric that was commonly used by the poor for various garments. It frequently lacked the iconic blue color, but it was essentially the same fabric. This would all change with another great turning point in American history, The Gold Rush, which began in 1849.

Levi Strauss went with his brothers, who owned a small store, west to California to sell goods to the many people flocking to California. They made a decent living but quickly found that what the miners really needed more than anything was good, sturdy pants. Mining and prospecting required spending long hours bent over or kneeling in the dirt, which was rough on their pants. Seeing as they generally didn't have a lot of money to start with, and prospecting in itself was costly, they didn't have the best quality pants.

Levi Strauss saw a solution. He began selling brown pants made from canvas duck, a medium to heavy-weight type of cotton. These weren't strong enough, so he swapped to denim. These proved much more popular, being harder-wearing and easier to repair when needed. Still, because the miners spent so much time kneeling and squatting, they had a tendency to pop the seams that held the pants together.

With a local tailor, Jacob Davis, who was already a regular customer, Strauss began to experiment. Strauss and Davis found that adding copper rivets to particular stress points prevented the seams from popping and kept the jeans in good shape for much longer. They patented their new invention in 1872, and jeans were born! Though many people came west in search of fortune in the form of gold nuggets, Strauss and his brothers made way more money than most prospectors through denim.

THE FIRST TRAIN ROBBERY

Imagine it: a steam engine pulling a long line of cars snakes its way through the American West. It chugs along steadily, climbing hills and winding across the Plains. Suddenly, a group of horsemen charges out of nowhere, bandanas on their faces and shooting their guns into the air. It's a quintessential image from popular imagination, and for good reason - train robberies are about as iconic to the Wild West as ten-gallon hats.

Funnily enough, the idea of robbing a train of its goods actually originated in Britain. The first recorded train robbery took place in 1855 on a train traveling between London and Folkestone. It was committed by several men who actually worked for the railroad; they knew the route and the security measures in place. The robbers very nearly got away with it, as they began melting down the gold bars they stole to create smaller amounts of gold that could be more easily sold.

Though they were eventually caught, the idea quickly caught on. Since so much transportation relied on trains in the American West, it was only natural that they became targeted. There were stretches where these trains had to go very slowly because of curves or steep hill grades, they passed through extremely isolated territory, and initially, there weren't any guards on board. Most importantly, they carried huge amounts of money to pay all of the workers who were employed out west for various companies, as there wasn't such a thing as a wire transfer that was reliable.

Unlike what you might see in movies, however, bandits rarely jumped onto moving trains - it was just way too dangerous and was likely to result in them getting squished under the train. Instead, the bandits would find a way to stop a train or board it under the guise of being a legitimate passenger. While safes were common targets after the advent of dynamite, robbing the passengers proved a faster and frequently more lucrative alternative. Without dynamite, the bandits had to rely on getting the combination to the safes from the company representatives on the trains, and they weren't always cooperative.

Like many things that are now thought of as being uniquely American, train robberies started overseas. Yet it was the rowdy bandits of the Wild West that quickly made it into an art all of their own.

CHARLES BOLES:
A GENTLEMAN BANDIT

Bandits and criminals of the Wild West are generally pictured as rough, tough, tobacco-spitting ruffians. This isn't completely without merit, as a lot of the men of the West were indeed such characters. There were some, however, that presented themselves entirely differently. Thus, the gentleman bandit was born.

Criminals being depicted as more than just bloodthirsty monsters out to make a buck was nothing new - the highwaymen of Europe had been romanticized for decades, possibly even centuries, by the time the Wild West was in its heyday. These tales of gentlemanly robbers possibly influenced some of the criminals in the West. One such fellow was Charles Boles, also known as Black Bart.

Not only was Charles Boles a very successful highwayman, making off with thousands of dollars, but he was also something of a character. He took to leaving poems at some of the scenes of his crimes, which a lot of people quickly assumed was his calling card. He was also extremely polite to the people he robbed, which was also highly unusual. This could have been a means to make people feel more at ease and therefore more cooperative, or it simply could have been how Boles conducted himself regardless of circumstances. He would wave a shotgun around, but never used it, which was also unusual.

Ironically, Boles was terrified of horses and avoided riding one whenever possible. He committed all of his robberies on foot, and then all of his getaways, too. Considering how many robberies he committed, it's astonishing that he managed to get away with it for so long.

Boles *was* eventually caught, but he was only convicted for his last known robbery. He was sentenced to six years in jail in 1884, but he only served four for his good behavior. All of the guards and law enforcement that dealt with Boles remarked that he was a very polite, witty, and well-spoken man who detested profanity. After his release, he performed one more spectacular escape: He evaded the press and curious citizens, then simply vanished without a trace. It's unknown with any certainty how Charles Boles spent his last days, proving that he really was one of the best in the business.

WOMEN ON THE FRONTIER

It's a pretty safe assumption to say that women in America in the 1800s didn't enjoy many personal freedoms. They couldn't own property except in special circumstances, they couldn't have their own bank account, and they were subject to a whole host of social rules that regulated everything from their behavior to how they dressed.

Though it may seem contrary, the wild environment of the western frontier of the United States offered a lot more in the way of freedom. Many women migrated with their families across the country and found themselves in a brave new world.

For instance, it became very commonplace, necessary even, for women to learn how to use firearms. In Europe and the eastern United States, it was only the very wealthy who learned how to shoot, and that was strictly for recreation. On the Great Plains, however, it was absolutely a skill that women needed for any number of reasons.

Because of the high death rates and lack of real laws regulating property ownership, women found themselves able to own property. This could be as simple as a single homestead or a massive cattle ranch. Several women grew to prominence as cattle barons or landladies. Nannita Daisey, called "Kentucky Daisey" by all who knew her, encouraged many women to participate in the Oklahoma land races, and entire communities of women sprung up.

Interestingly, because women were commonly landowners and the laws weren't written yet, this also allowed them to vote in elections. Wyoming Territory was the first to have women voters in 1869. Decades before the fight for American suffrage began, the women of the West were the first to enjoy voting rights in the United States. Not only that, but many of them would go on to serve in public office.

Even seemingly small freedoms, such as wearing pants, were accepted. On the frontier, it was far more important to get on with the work of keeping ranches, farms, and growing towns running than to worry about whether women were wearing the correct kind of skirt - or any skirt at all!

THE SHIPWRECK THAT CAUSED
A GLOBAL FINANCIAL CRISIS

Everyone knows that there were piles of gold unearthed during the California Gold Rush of 1849 and onward. What most people don't realize, however, is just how essential that gold was in keeping the American economy working as it should. Without it, banking and trade wouldn't be possible.

In the first half of the 19th century, there wasn't such a thing as a central bank, like there is today. Gold was necessary as a means to back American currency. This meant that gold had to get all the way from California to the East Coast, where many of the banking institutions were, and of course, the government offices, too. While it could be shipped by railroad, this was considered dangerous due to the long overland route and the possibility of bandits. Ships were the preferred method of transportation, especially with the new paddle steamers.

One such ship, the *SS Central America*, was one of the most expensive ever built, costing $140,000 at the time. It was worth it though, for she had a side-paddle wheel, and was much faster than sail-powered ships. On September 3, 1857, the *SS Central America* departed from port in Panama and began steaming her way north to New York with 477 passengers and 101 crew.

Unfortunately, she ran smack into a strong hurricane and began to flounder. About 100 people, mostly women and children, were put into lifeboats to transfer to other nearby ships. In the end, *SS Central America* sank and took 425 souls with her. She also took her cargo to the bottom of the sea: over nine *tons* of solid gold. This was worth about $8,000,000 at the time, or around $288,000,000 as of 2024.

This gold was badly needed to shore up the growing American economy and to allow banks to continue to trade with customers. When news of the sinking reached the mainland, there was a panic, and banks began to fail. This devastated local economies and damaged the national economy, too. The United States entered a Depression that didn't truly abate until after the Civil War.

DID YOU KNOW?

○ The first quickdraw gunfight occurred on July 21, 1865, between Bill Hickock and Davis Tutt after a personal dispute. Hickock was the victor.

○ Despite their prevalence in movies and TV shows, the iconic ten-gallon hats were actually not popular at all. The most common style of hat in the West was a flat-brimmed Stetson.

○ Wyatt Earp's fame is largely due to him being one of the few survivors of the Wild West era, and because he went on to become a consultant for Western films in the early days of Hollywood.

○ The first armed bank robbery was committed by a postmaster who was deeply in debt. He entered a bank while drunk and made off with $5,000.

○ The first Western movie every released was *The Great Train Robbery*, though the actor was not a cowboy at all - he was the son of a traveling salesman and longed for a life of adventure, so renamed himself "Bronco Bill Anderson" and pretended he was a cowboy.

CHAPTER 11:
MODERN HISTORY

SOUTH AFRICA'S NUCLEAR DISARMAMENT

For much of the 20th century, many nations engaged in a policy of "mutually assured destruction." This was largely due to the divisions of the Cold War. The thinking was that open conflict could (hopefully) be avoided by knowing that should any nation be attacked; the instigator would be destroyed as well. It was a strange notion, using weapons of mass destruction for peace.

In such a political climate, it's easy to see why so many countries around the world wanted to be as armed as possible. There were some, however, that chose a different path. One of the most interesting examples of this is South Africa and its path to disarmament.

Like many nations in the wake of the Allied victory that was partially achieved through using nuclear weapons, South Africa quickly began the work to establish their own nuclear program. They were successful and soon had several warheads. In addition to this, they began to develop delivery methods as well, including warcraft built specifically for this purpose.

Throughout the 20th century, the geopolitical climate was shifting, though, and many nations underwent radical changes. This was especially true on the African continent, with European nations, such as the United Kingdom, relinquishing their colonies. Additionally, there was much social upheaval in the form of coups and, in South Africa, the fight against apartheid.

The government of South Africa had a startling realization as they watched nations around them, and indeed around the entire world undergoing some of these changes. Though they had created their nuclear weapons program as a means of determent, there was no telling what another government might do with them should the country undergo a revolution or military coup in the future. It was to this end that South Africa sought to end its program, becoming one of the only nations in the whole world to do so voluntarily.

Today, South Africa's supply of uranium is being transformed into medical isotopes to help research and fight diseases.

VINE-GLO AND THE VERY HELPFUL WARNING LABEL

The American experiment with Prohibition in the 1920s was complicated at best. It led to a huge uptick in crime, and most Americans were opposed to it for one reason or another. Though it was illegal to buy or sell alcoholic beverages, this didn't stop many people from finding a way around this ban, as it wasn't illegal to *drink* alcohol.

The liquor industry was obviously devastated during Prohibition, which did nothing to help the pending Great Depression that would cripple the economy. To stay afloat, many companies that had previously been producing alcoholic beverages turned to other means of turning a profit, leading to a boom in creativity. Vine-Glo was one innovation that resulted.

Sold by Fruit Industries, Vine-Glo was a relatively simple product. It was more or less simply a brick of dehydrated grapes and sugar, sort of like a brick of fruit leather. It's intended purpose was to be a means of making grape juice at home. The fact that it came in eight varieties, all of them based on wine flavors, was just a happy coincidence, and definitely, absolutely, for sure not intentional.

Likewise, Vine-Glo came with a very important (and informative) warning label. See, it doesn't really take a whole lot of effort to turn grapes and sugar into wine, so long as you follow some basic steps. As this was the era of Prohibition, it was illegal to produce alcoholic beverages, but what citizens did in their own homes was largely considered their own business, so long as they didn't attempt to sell it. The fact that Vine-Glo's warning label was essentially a step-by-step instruction list on how to turn their product into wine was totally unrelated…, right?

Supporters of Prohibition attempted to shut down Vine-Glo's production a number of times, but the government ruled in Vine-Glo's favor. The agents of the Bureau of Prohibition were strictly prohibited from stopping its shipments or delaying them in any way. In fact, the Assistant Attorney General at the time, Mabel Walker Willebrandt, would go on to become an attorney for Fruit Industries, the company that produced Vine-Glo.

WINSTON CHURCHILL AND FDR'S BATHTIME CONVERSATION

It's no secret that the United States and the United Kingdom enjoyed a very special relationship during World War II. When the United States entered the war in 1941, there was a great shift not only in the actual war but also in public sentiment, especially in war-weary Britain. This close comradery was fostered in no small part by the tight working relationship between Franklin D. Roosevelt and Winston Churchill.

When it became patently obvious that the United States had been thrust into the war by the surprise attack on Pearl Harbor, Winston Churchill immediately began to plan a visit to the White House. In fact, he sent the request on December 8, 1941, the very next day after the attack. FDR agreed to host the Prime Minister and welcomed him only two weeks later.

The two enjoyed a close, friendly relationship, frequently staying up late to drink and smoke cigars. They would watch movies together in their downtime, and Churchill would frequently lounge about the White House in his pajamas, holding informal audiences with Roosevelt at any hour of the day. He even wheeled Roosevelt's wheelchair on occasion. The fact that Roosevelt even required a wheelchair was a carefully concealed secret, something that the president and his staff went to great lengths to keep from the public.

Churchill and Roosevelt's close relationship led to them frequently exchanging ideas whenever they came. On one such occasion, FDR hit upon the perfect name for the Allies and their commitment to universal victory: "A Declaration by the United

Nations." Roosevelt, excited by the concept of nations being united in a single purpose, wheeled himself directly to Churchill's suite of rooms.

Unknown to Roosevelt, Churchill took long baths to help with his own health problems and was engaged in doing just that. When the president entered, Churchill was standing there, completely naked, having just exited the bathroom. Roosevelt naturally tried to apologize, but Churchill simply said, "The Prime Minister of Great Britain has nothing to hide from the President of the United States."

CAT SPIES

People like to imagine international spies using all sorts of cool gadgets and toys to complete adrenaline-fueled secret missions. This is definitely what Hollywood has told us, at any rate. Truth is often stranger than fiction, however, and this was definitely true during the Cold War.

Both sides were equally paranoid about listening devices, so they had to get more and more creative with how they spied on one another. This also meant that they became more and more paranoid about how they were being spied *on*. Because of this, they resorted to some strange means of gathering intelligence. This meant recruiting even the most unexpected spies: animals, more specifically, cats.

There were several attempts to use animals for spying that didn't work for one reason or another. Dogs were too friendly and obvious, rats were too small and unreliable, and birds were too flighty and prone to going outside of transmission range. The CIA landed on one particular species as the best candidate: cats.

Now, everyone knows that cats are difficult to train at the best of times, so sending one on a secret mission probably seems like a fool's errand. Nevertheless, the CIA recruited veterinarians and scientists to collaborate on a way for cats to be used for this very purpose. A tiny microphone was planted in a cat's ear canal, a radio transmitter at the bottom of its skull near the neck, and a very thin wire into its fur. The setup needed to not only appear normal but also be undetectable if someone petted the cat.

The goal was to be able to use these furry little spies to observe and transmit information from Soviet embassies, and possibly even directly from the Kremlin itself. The first test was to have the initial test cat released just outside of the Soviet embassy at a nearby park, where embassy staff sometimes liked to sit and chat together.

Unfortunately, this project proved to be a complete failure - cats were simply too hard to train. They would frequently blow their cover by scratching at the implanted equipment or simply being too friendly to be mistaken for a stray. Sometimes they would simply wander off! The project was scrapped, all equipment was removed from the cat spy, and it went on to live a cushy retirement.

THE OREGON TRAIL ON PAPER

The well-known computer game *The Oregon Trail* was a staple of many people's childhoods. Many of us have fond memories of sitting in the school computer lab and booting it up, spending hours traveling the trail only to die of dysentery. Given its popularity as a computer game, it might be surprising to learn that, originally, it wasn't one at all.

In the 1970s, computers were still pretty unknown in terms of their uses and potential uses. The concept of a "home computer" was still decades away. Even so, many schools around the country were eager to try and implement them into their curriculum. This was an important step, as computers were quickly being adapted into the workplace, and children would need to understand them for future employment. Even so, most of their experience with computers was through arcade-style video games.

The Oregon Trail was created in this environment. What is less well-known, however, is the fact that it wasn't originally intended to be a computer game at all. Don Rawitsch, one of the three creators, was working as a student teacher in a small Minnesota school. He had been assigned by his supervising teacher to cover the history chapter on the westward expansion of the United States.

Rawitsch had been observing how classes were taught for a few weeks, and he was not super impressed with the traditional method of giving students information, and then having them repeat it back through either tests or reports. He believed that there was a way to incorporate fun into learning. With that in mind, he created a simple board game on a roll of paper. This paper could be rolled or unrolled, sort of like a computer screen scrolling, to show progress along the Oregon Trail, one of the most popular routes for settlers to take across the western frontier.

There were already elements of the original game that would become recognizable in the computer version that most of us know today, such as travelers in the party having an assigned role, having to carefully manage supplies, and making decisions that could affect the success of the trip.

It was only when Rawitsch's roommates, Bill Heinemann and Paul Dillenberger saw what he was doing that they realized that it would make the perfect game to run on the new personal computers. Thus, a legend was born.

THE FLAT TIRE THAT FOUND A DINOSAUR

One of the most exciting exhibits to see at a museum is dinosaur fossils. As they tower overhead, it's hard to imagine a time when they roamed the Earth, and an elephant would have seemed small in comparison. For such large critters, it can be surprisingly difficult to locate their remains. In fact, a good number of them are discovered purely by accident. Such is the case for one of the most fossils in the world: Sue, the Tyrannosaurus Rex.

In 1990, Sue Hendrickson had been working with a team in South Dakota to see if they could uncover any fossils. The area had proved to be rich with them in the past, and it proved to be a fruitful summer. The team discovered several samples of Edmontasaurus bones, and it was considered a successful dig already. They were preparing to leave on August 12, ready to take their fossils back to the Black Hills Institute to study them.

Fate intervened then, and it was discovered that the team's truck had a flat tire. While some of the team decided to go into the local town to see if they could get it repaired, some others stayed behind to continue packing up. Sue, however, decided to go exploring around the area. Sue was a very adventurous lady, having done everything from lobster fishing to amber mining, and even salvaging by diving on shipwrecks. So, it was perfectly natural for her to set off across the rugged terrain just to see what she could see.

It proved to be a great idea, for Sue stumbled across some small pieces of bone at the bottom of a cliff. She quickly established that they must have come from the cliff above her - erosion had exposed them and caused some of the smaller ones to fall down. She reported the discovery, and it was determined that they were T-rex bones. Sue and a few members of the team stayed behind and began to work to excavate them.

Their efforts were rewarded: the T-rex, nicknamed "Sue" for her finder, has the unique distinction of being the most complete T-rex fossil ever found. In fact, Sue, the T-rex had over 90% of her bones recovered, as well as a complete skull. If not for a simple flat tire, this amazing discovery might never have been found!

DID YOU KNOW?

○ On September 26, 1983, Stanislav Petrov, watch commander in the Soviet Union's early nuclear missile warning system, chose not to report the launch of five US missiles. This was a good decision since the missile was just a cloud the warning satellite had detected!

○ Nintendo, now famous for making video games and consoles, was founded in 1889 and originally produced playing cards.

○ Bubble wrap, used in all kinds of packaging today, was invented in 1957 as a textured wallpaper intended to appeal to the nontraditional young adults of the Beat Generation.

○ A typical smartphone in 2020 had over 100,000 times the processor speed, and over 1,000,000 times the RAM, of the *Apollo 11* moon lander's guidance computer in 1969. Even when compared to the total computer power of NASA in 1969, the smartphone is still way more powerful.

○ During the Cold War, the USSR thought that the heavily trafficked building in the center of the courtyard of the Pentagon was a top-secret building. The USSR targeted this area and almost dropped nuclear weapons on the building before finding out that it was a hot dog stand!

CHAPTER 12:
MEDIEVAL HISTORY

CRUSADES TATTOOS

Tattoos have a long and rich history across a variety of cultures. Conversely, they also have a long history of being taboo in particular circles. Many religions have rules against them, particularly some Christian denominations. Ironically, there was a time when it was not only possible to get tattoos as a medieval Christian, but even celebrated.

The Crusades were a long series of wars waged by various European nations on the Muslims that controlled Jerusalem at the time. The Pope (many Popes, in fact) encouraged noblemen and even kings and princes to go on Crusade, that is, to make a pilgrimage that was also a war campaign. This was extremely expensive, to say nothing of the huge amount of danger involved. Everything from disease and storms at sea while traveling, to the actual fighting itself made these journeys exceedingly risky. It was only natural, then, that those who survived the ordeal would want to commemorate their perilous journey.

Though tattoos may seem very modern, a surprising number of medieval people sported body art. This wasn't always limited to tattoos: Scarification, branding, and other body modifications were all practiced by various sects and artists in Jerusalem and in other places on the way to the Holy City.

Crusaders adopted this from the Coptic Christians, who had a practice of tattooing a cross on themselves, typically the inside of the wrist or forearm, as a way to prove their faith and devotion. Much like how tourists today like to bring souvenirs home, knights on Crusade would come home with fresh ink. Despite the many taboos against other forms of tattooing, this was seen as not only okay, but flat-out worthy of being celebrated. It wasn't only knights that came home sporting new ink - it was monarchs, too. King Harold II of England had a score of tattoos, which would prove useful when it came time to identify his body after the Battle of Hastings in 1066.

PUBLIC BATHHOUSES

When you think of the so-called Middle Ages, you probably think of poor peasants with dingy clothes and smudged faces, right? After all, it's not like they had indoor plumbing, so they must have been filthy and smelled terrible all the time - it only makes sense. Well, this is actually wildly untrue, despite what you might see in movies and TV series.

Cleanliness was of great concern throughout history; at no point has any human society ever reveled in the idea of being dirty. This was especially true in the medieval period. For starters, they wore linen, which is naturally anti-microbial and exfoliates the skin as it's worn. The layer they wore closest to the body would be washed and boiled rigorously, not only to maintain its color but for health too. There were even specific instructions published on how to wash yourself in the cleanest manner possible.

To this end, there were also public bathhouses across Europe. Most people associate public bathing with the Romans, which is fair. However, after the fall of the Roman Empire, this tradition continued in many locations. In places where it lacked, like in Britain, it underwent a great revival under Christianity. Church elders encouraged rigorous bathing for hygiene and to help curb diseases. They even went so far as to build bathhouses near pilgrimage sites and along their routes. Bathhouses were even found in monasteries.

In fact, one of the duties of the clergy was to maintain hot baths for the poor. Even the pope was known to sponsor these efforts, sometimes even allowing the use of his luxurious baths in his private residences. Some orders would even go so far as to run what we would recognize as a spa.

It wasn't just the Catholic Church that encouraged bathing - it was also lay people. Crusaders would encounter bathhouses on their journey to and from Jerusalem and would bring the custom back to Europe. Unfortunately, by the 1500s, many of these bathhouses had devolved into little more than brothels, and many were shut down during the Restoration.

STRANGE WALKING SHOES

Clothing from the past can seem really strange to our modern eyes. Despite their strange outward appearance, however, most of these garments served at least some kind of practical reason. That being said, it's really hard to see the practical reason behind some things, like the *poulaines*, those medieval shoes with the really long toes.

This style of shoe came and went several times from about 1200–1500. The length of the toe would vary by region and time. No matter the length, however, it was necessary to stuff the toe to maintain the proper shape and to keep it from collapsing. Sometimes it was even necessary to fix the toe to the shin by a small silver chain so that it was even remotely possible to walk in it.

Even with shorter toes, it was impossible to walk normally in poulaines. The soles, like other shoes of the period, were made of soft leather, which already meant that people had to walk with a lighter step than we typically do today. Add in a ridiculously long toe, and walking in the normal heel-toe fashion became flat-out impossible. Instead, people would put the ball of the foot down first and sort of skate along if the floor was smooth enough. Outdoors, they would maintain most of the weight on the ball of the foot, with the heel coming down only lightly.

This strange style of walking led to a lot of people developing really muscular calves. This fit well into the fashion of wearing short pants or breeches with wool or silk stockings. A lot of the gestures and postures of courtly life or upper society centered around the legs and placement thereof. For instance, the polite way of bowing to a monarch at many courts was to place one foot forward and to bend the back leg, while bowing with the upper body.

This style of shoe wasn't without its critics, however. Many churchmen complained that men couldn't bow properly during services because of their absurdly toed shoes. King Charles V of France even banned them from not just being worn, but from even being made in Paris!

DOG-POWERED COOKING SPITS

It's probably not exactly news to anyone that before the advent of modern appliances, household tasks were way more difficult and took longer. Cooking was obviously no exception. Making meals took a massive time investment that couldn't really be avoided. Even so, humans have always been inventive, so they came up with an ingenious solution to help save some time: turnspit dogs.

Ovens as we think of them today weren't really common for most households in the medieval era. Most houses had only a central fire pit that provided light, warmth, and a place to cook. Even those homes that had actual hearths weren't particularly well-suited to the sort of cooking that we do today. Therefore, the most popular method to cook large pieces of meat (a real luxury) was to roast it on a spit.

This was *real* roasting, not what most people call roasting today but is actually baking. The meat would be put on a metal spit, and then it would be slowly turned while hung over a fire, being basted the whole time so that it would be flavorful and wouldn't burn. Naturally, this meant a huge time investment - the spit had to be constantly turning, or the meat would burn, or at the very least, cook unevenly. That meant that one member of the household would have to sit and do only that, which is hardly an efficient use of time.

Enter the turnspit dog! This was a scrappy little breed of dog that was bred just for this task. They had long, strong bodies, and short legs. These tiny beasts of burden would be put into a wooden wheel that they were just the right size for, and then they would be encouraged to walk so the wheel would turn. The wooden wheel was attached to the cooking spit via a leather strap or sometimes actual gears in the walls, and the meat would therefore keep turning.

This method persisted up until the 18th century and possibly as late as the 19th century in some parts of the world. Even after spit roasting fell out of favor, turnspit dogs found jobs working in other ways, such as turning wheels in apothecaries that were connected to devices to make pills. Queen Victoria herself adopted some retired turnspit dogs.

EELS: MEDIEVAL CURRENCY

Trade and commerce have always been an integral part of society. No matter the time or culture, people find a way to trade goods for what they need. Money, be it coinage or banknotes, largely replaced the bartering system. This has sometimes fallen out of favor, especially if the local currency is unstable or unreliable. Sometimes it was simply a case of there not being enough physical money to go around because production was so slow.

This was the case in medieval England. Minting coins was a long, complicated process. It didn't help that every time a new king was crowned, new coins had to be minted, which included designing, smelting, and finishing them. Given that this was a period of political turmoil, it's little wonder that coins were in short supply. Moreover, the value of the coins could fluctuate wildly depending on a number of factors. Sometimes people would engage in a practice known as "coin clipping," where they would snip off the edges of the coins, then melt these bits down and use them to make new coins. This could cause inflation, or sometimes the king would declare that new coins had to be minted to combat this problem.

Naturally, it was usually more convenient to pay via bartering or with goods. A lot of landlords would accept payment in the form of grain, wool, flour, or whatever else was at hand. These are all fairly normal items that one would expect peasants to have, right? Well, as it turns out, there was one thing that was even more popular to use as currency: eels!

Eels were popular as a food because of the Lenten prohibition against meat, and eels (much like other seafood) weren't considered meat at the time. The idea was that land-based meat made people feel amorous, and that was strictly to be avoided during Lent. Eels were encouraged as a meal, and the people responded happily. Smoked, salted, pickled, or any kind of preserved eel was acceptable as a trade good or form of currency. This was so popular that, during the 11th century, over 500,000 eels were being used to pay rent annually!

THE ORIGINS OF
THE UPPER CRUST

Some phrases seem like they've been with us forever. Referring to the upper classes or something nice or expensive as "upper crust" is one of those. If you think about it, it doesn't make a whole lot of sense - no one really wants to be referred to as a *crust*, surely. Surprisingly, we know exactly how this particular phrase began, and there is actually a logic to it.

During the medieval period, as mentioned previously, most homes didn't have an oven that could be baked in. If they did have an oven, it really wasn't big enough to handle all the baking that was required, since bread formed most of a peasant's diet. Most, if not all, communities had a bakehouse where citizens could come and leave their bread dough, cakes, pies, or whatever else to be baked. More often than not, these bakehouses were in monasteries or convents.

These religious institutions were sort of like local tax collectors a lot of the time. They would take a portion of the goods that the local farmers and other peasants created. This could be anything from wool to candles to grain, even ground flour. This was necessary to keep the monasteries working.

The nuns or monks would take charge of the bread, too, and they would keep a portion of it for themselves in payment for baking it. The poorer people would have their bread dough made from rougher, darker grains, while the wealthier noblemen (local knights, lords, etc.) would have purer, whiter flour. The baking itself was not an exact science - it wasn't like they had reliable timers or thermostats, after all.

The fire used to heat the ovens was always covered in soot, too, as the fire that heated the ovens had to be built directly in it, and then scraped out. Dough would be placed directly on the bottom of the oven, so when it was done baking, it would have a dirty, sooty bottom crust. Being that most people in the medieval period were quite poor, they naturally couldn't afford to throw any part of the bread away, so they'd just eat it as-is. The wealthy people of the community, however, would slice off this bottom portion, and only eat the "upper crust." That was the start of referring to more expensive or nicer things as "upper crust!"

DID YOU KNOW?

○ Animal trials were a thing in the medieval period. They would be arrested and go through a trial if they committed a "crime," usually killing a human.

○ Britain had a relatively weak army and few funds to pay for professional soldiers, so archery practice was mandatory weekly for every able-bodied man.

○ It was extremely rare for peasants to work outside of their homes. Even if they weren't farmers, they worked in their own homes as weavers, candlemakers, etc.

○ One of the most common dishes to eat was a "perpetual soup." Since starting a fire took a lot of work and fuel, and it was even *more* work and fuel to get a pot hot enough to cook in, most were left on the fire and continually boiled. Additional ingredients would just be added every day.

○ It was fashionable throughout the medieval period in different European countries for women to pluck their hairlines to make their foreheads look larger. This fashion last came into style during the reign of Elizabeth I of England.

CHAPTER 13:
SPORTS

THE ROYAL SOCCER BAN

Soccer (or football, depending on where in the world you are) is one of the most popular sports in the world. There are thousands of clubs, teams, and associations, and it's a multi-billion-dollar industry. There are even soccer video games if you just can't get enough soccer in your life. The sport wasn't always that popular, however; in fact, it was downright loathed and even banned at various points in history.

Though the exact origins of soccer are debated, it was clearly already an established sport by the 14th century. The trouble was, there really wasn't such a thing as a dedicated sporting field. The only reserved parcels of land for such an activity were parks for hunting. This meant that players had to play wherever they could, which wasn't always very convenient. This was especially true in London.

The population of London swelled quickly between 1200 and 1500, going from just a few thousand to hundreds of thousands. City planning wasn't really a concept yet, so people were crammed into the city cheek by jowl. The streets themselves were a twisting, confusing warren, with some of them narrowing suddenly into corners that could be impossible to navigate with a horse and cart. Compounding the problem was the fact that the narrower streets were sometimes just roofed over and became rookeries, or dens where the poor congregated.

So, London wasn't really an ideal location for a soccer game at the best of times. There weren't any public parks, and every inch of space was needed, especially with the rising merchant class. On April 13, 1314, King Edward II had enough. He banned soccer outright, citing the "great noise" and "many evils which may arise" from the sport, though it was also largely due to complaints from merchants.

He was not the last monarch to attempt to ban the sport: Edward III, IV, Richard II, Henry IV, and Henry VIII all attempted to outlaw soccer as well, all without much success.

HOT AIR BALLOONS
AT THE OLYMPICS

The Olympic Games are a celebration of pretty much every kind of sport known to humankind. They're meant to be a display of the athleticism and competitive spirit of the best that a nation has to offer. In the early 20th century, the modern Olympics weren't really established - many features we consider obvious parts of the Olympics now weren't in practice yet.

Though many nations had attempted to revive the ancient Greek Olympics since at least the 1600s, these had been more of a regional affair. Truly international Olympic games, overseen by the International Olympic Committee, didn't begin until 1896. This was pretty much unknown territory, and there was a great deal of debate as to what should and shouldn't be included. Despite initial enthusiasm, after these initial games there was also a bit of a slump in their popularity, as well as questions about their prestige and legitimacy.

To add more spectacles and draw in more crowds, the IOC decided to add some events designed to draw a crowd. Specifically, they included hot air ballooning. Though manned balloon flights had existed since the late 18th century, the idea of flight had really captured the public imagination in 1900. This was only a few years before the Wright brothers' famous flight, after all, and aviation was very popular in France. As the games were to be hosted in Paris, his seemed like a natural fit.

So, balloonists gathered at the 1900 Olympics. There wasn't an official race, per se, but there were many categories in which balloonists could be awarded: distance, duration, elevation, target without stop (making it to a destination without a refuel or rest stop), target with stop, and distance and duration overall. Given the great effort needed to transport hot air balloons internationally at the time, it's hardly surprising that most, if not all, of the winners were French.

The Games of 1900 was the first and last time hot air balloonists competed at the Olympics, owing mostly to the complicated nature of judging and logistics of transporting the balloons themselves.

BOWLING:
THE SPORT OF KINGS?

When you imagine royal pastimes, activities like jousting or hunting probably come to mind, and maybe horse racing of some sort as well, right? While these are all absolutely the purview of monarchs, they aren't the only sports that have caught the royal eye. In fact, it may surprise you to learn that bowling - yes, bowling - was once the favorite sport of kings, or at least one in particular.

Though he's known for other, less salubrious things, King Henry VIII of England was renowned for his athleticism in the first half of his reign. He enjoyed sports of all varieties and was known throughout Europe for being a great athlete with grace and skill. Many of his palaces had facilities for sports built on the grounds, and bowling was no exception.

Henry was so taken with bowling that not only did he have his own private lanes built at Whitehall Palace, but he also made bowling an exclusively upper-class sport. It was flat-out illegal for commoners to bowl as of 1511. In 1541, he also passed a law that stated that commoners could only bowl on Christmas Day, and that was only at the home of their lord or master, and he had to supervise.

Rules regulating who could and couldn't play was about the only thing standard about the game for a long time. The number of pins could vary wildly from three to 17, and the size and material of the balls and pins differed as well. In fact, it was Martin Luther (the originator of the Protestant Reformation) who reportedly set the standard number of pins at ten. He had a private lane built next to his house and would allegedly play with his children.

The lanes themselves were also quite different from what we see in modern bowling alleys. Instead of being perfectly flat and smooth, they were built like a ditch with high sides. The bowler was expected to use these high sides, curving the ball around to hit the pins. It was a very different experience from what we're used to today - but at least we don't have to bowl under the watchful eye of a king!

THE FIRST NASCAR PRIZE WAS NO PRIZE

It's no secret that today, NASCAR is a multibillion-dollar industry. The drivers and racing teams themselves have the chance to pull in millions of dollars from prizes alone. This wasn't always the case, however - NASCAR prizes were originally much smaller, a reflection of its humble origins.

Stock car racing has its origins in bootlegging in the 1920s and early 1930s. Bootleggers would compete to see who could make their deliveries the fastest, with better drivers getting better deals. With the repeal of Prohibition in 1933, there were a lot of really skilled drivers with modified cars on the backroads of the United States without any way to show their prowess. Small, local races began to be organized, which quickly became centered around Daytona Beach.

Though originally tracks for testing cars, especially regarding speed, were generally in Europe, Daytona Beach quickly replaced them as the place to try for land speed records. It was flat and open, the perfect setting. Though there was also a stretch of asphalt road, the sand was an integral part of the track to test drivers' skills as well as how the cars performed.

Though an informal race had occurred in 1936 to determine the best driver in the nation, it wasn't until 1947 that an official race was organized. Originally called the National Championship Stock Car Circuit, or NCSCC, the first season was held in 1947 and lasted nearly the entire year. Tracks covered a variety of terrains, including dirt. These efforts were headed by Bill France, who had been at that initial race in 1936.

Despite their enthusiasm for the event, it proved impossible to gain a sponsor, not least of which because this style of racing was seen as somewhat disreputable. Though it may seem strange to think of now, given that sponsors clamor over each other to participate in NASCAR, the foundling organization had a real cash flow problem.

Undeterred, Bill France fundraised and committed some of his own money to the prize. At the end of the 1947 season, $1,000 was distributed to the winner along with a trophy. As of 2024, this was the equivalent of just over $14,000, a far cry from the millions up for grabs today.

THE GREAT AMERICAN PASTIME - OR NOT

Ah, baseball - is there anything so quintessentially American? Sitting under the sun on a summer day, eating a hotdog, and watching a game is such a uniquely American experience that it's become a kind of cultural shorthand for the United States and is instantly recognizable. We even refer to baseball as "the Great American Pastime." This is actually a bit of a misnomer. Though it was no doubt adopted and perfected by Americans, its origins are decidedly not.

People have been playing stick-and-ball games for about as long as humans have been able to hold and swing sticks. Nearly every culture across the world has some kind of game with some of these elements. Even laundresses in the time before washing machines were known to hit "soap nuts," or little balls of soap, with their wooden laundry paddles in their limited downtime. Therefore, the earliest origins of the sport can prove a little elusive.

What *is* known is that by the 18th century, many baseball-like games were popular in Britain. Two of the most popular were "rounders" and an early form of baseball, though these may have just been regional varieties of the same game. Considering that we still refer to someone as "rounding" the bases on the baseball diamond, this seems entirely likely.

The very first recorded game of baseball (referred to as "bass-ball") took place in 1744 in Surrey, England. This was no ordinary game, for it featured Frederick, the Prince of Wales and oldest son of King George II of Great Britain, as a player. For a member of the royal family to participate indicates that it was not only an established sport but one enjoyed by the upper classes. This was a far cry from the rough-and-tumble game enjoyed by children.

From England, baseball appears to have been brought not to America, but to Canada, by English immigrants. From there, it naturally traveled down to what would become the United States. So, not only is baseball originally British, but Canada had the sport before the US!

LITTLE HORSES
WITH LOTS OF HEART

There's no mistaking a thoroughbred racehorse: tall and sleek, with long legs and athletic bodies. They're well-tuned athletes, perfectly adapted to their sport. Though their size can vary greatly, they generally are known for being a taller breed of horse, averaging about 16 hands tall (a hand is a unit of measurement that equals four inches) at their withers, or the top of the shoulders or neck. It's strange to think, then, that there was a time when they were considerably smaller.

The thoroughbred as a breed is relatively recent when compared to some others that have been around since time immemorial. In fact, it was one of these ancient breeds that provided the foundations of the thoroughbred: the Arabian horse. All modern thoroughbred racehorses can trace their lineage to three stallions that were imported to England in the 1600s and 1700s. Other stallions were imported, but these three proved to be the most significant.

While these stallions brought endurance, speed, and a drive to win and love of running to the breed, they did *not* bring height. Arabian horses, as a general rule, tend to be small and finely built. This was compounded by the fact that the British mares to which these imported stallions were bred were also quite small, as large horses for riding were generally out of favor. British racehorses were small also because longer races were the norm, and large horses tend to tire quicker than smaller ones.

All of this is to say that thoroughbreds were originally about 13.5 hands tall, about the size of a modern pony. It's hard to think about these little horses pelting down a racetrack, but they proved unstoppable. They had a desire to run and better build than the stockier British breeds that had been raced previously. Breeders quickly began to select for height - within two generations, the offspring were sprouting up to 16 hands tall - and the rest is history. The tall, graceful thoroughbred we know today was born.

DID YOU KNOW?

○ Super Bowl referees are awarded rings just like the winning team, though theirs are smaller and more subtle.

○ Though some sports including in the Olympic Games have proven controversial, what about the fine arts that were included from 1912–1948, before finally being discontinued in 1954?

○ In 1971, *Apollo 14* astronauts Alan Shephard and Edgar Mitchell made history when they became the first people to play sports on the moon. Shephard hit a golf ball while Mitchell threw a makeshift javelin, which was actually a staff they'd used in one of their scientific experiments.

○ Not just the plot of a comedic movie, the tropical nation of Jamaica have graced the Winter Olympics with a bobsled team eight times since their debut in 1988, with a women's team joining the men in 2018.

○ The longest recorded boxing match with gloves was between Andy Bowen and Jack at New Orleans, Louisiana, USA on April 6, 1893. It lasted 110 rounds, seven hours, and 19 minutes (9:15 p.m.-4:34 a.m.), and it was declared a no contest (later changed to a draw).

CONCLUSION

This book has hopefully been as educational as it was entertaining. The world is indeed a strange place, and humans have contributed in no small part to that strangeness. From the very oldest points in human history to the modern age, human existence has been a fascinating tapestry of shared experiences.

If nothing else, this book should have opened your eyes to what a wonderful place the world is and how full it is of stories beyond the expected. It was written with a love of learning and a fervent hope that it will inspire some sort of curiosity or investigation on your part.

No matter if you're a casual reader or someone who just likes trivia, this book was intended for anyone who has a desire to learn. This book itself is a celebration of curiosity, meant to feed a hunger for knowledge.

Nothing would be more pleasing than to know that maybe, just maybe, something in these pages sparked an interest, and you've decided to go learn more about it. At the very least, perhaps this book will help you to dominate at the next trivia night, or at least gives you some fun anecdotes to amuse your friends, family, or co-workers.

Thank you for coming along on this long, strange trip throughout history and across cultures - we hope it was fun, educational, and maybe just a little weird, too!

13045471R00105